The Top

Tower

Air Fryer

Cookbook For Beginners

2023

1000 Days Quick and Affordable Air Fryer Recipes Anyone Can Easily Learn incl. Side Dishes, Desserts, Snacks and More

Adolfo Stark

Warning-Disclaimer

The purpose of this book is to educate and entertain. The author or publisher does not guarantee that anyone following the techniques, suggestions, tips, ideas, or strategies will become successful. The author and publisher shall have neither liability or responsibility to anyone with respect to any loss or damage caused, or alleged to be caused, directly or indirectly by the information contained in this book.

Table of Contents

Chapter 8 Fish and Seafood 48

Chapter 9 Beef, Pork, and Lamb.. 53

Chapter 10 Desserts 60

INTRODUCTION

The word Air Fryer has quickly become the buzz word of the year following on from the covid-19 pandemic, we're all looking for a quick and easy way to cook! Before purchasing an air fryer, I remember feeling like a total beginner in the kitchen but having one has really stepped up my cooking game! When it comes to cooking, it's important to never cut corner, especially when it comes to flavour but there are many tricks that I've learnt over the years for saving time when cooking – having an Air Fryer has helped a lot!

When I think of fast meals, I'm often reminded of the mayhem of trying to get to a 9am meeting when it's 8:55am and you've barely made it out of the house with children, lunchboxes and car keys flying everywhere – knowing full well it'll take you a lot longer than 5 minutes to get to the meeting! Having an Air Fryer makes the mayhem a little less chaotic at dinner time and brings a lot of peace and calm back into our dinner time routine.

Whilst the usual morning mayhem is often out of our control, what is not out of our control is the food we cook from our kitchens. From the meals cooked in large quantities when expecting extra family guests, the evening dinners for the kids or the weekend cake baked ready for a whole afternoon of relaxing. That's what I know I can control – and so can you!

Together let's take ownership of the kitchen once more and explore the world of air fryers.

Chapter 1 Tower Air Fryer Basic Guide

There's no denying that after the recent lockdowns, there was a surge in air fryers but you might just be wondering what exactly an air fryer is! The term can often be quite confusing; frying foods without air just does not make any sense meaning that lots of people are usually put off from purchasing one due to being so unsure on how it all works.

Tower has the largest range of Air Fryers and always promises to meet all of your air frying needs. Towe Air Fryers are they ONLY Air Fryer brands to come with Vortx Technology as they cook 30% faster than others to help you create meals that a almost completely fat free!

How Does the Tower Air Fryer Work?

The Air Fryer itself is similar to an oven as a small convention appliance which cooks in exactly the same way that an oven does, with a small fan that circulates hot air at high temperatures – cooking food in a similar way to frying without submersing the food in oil!

Air Fryers are quite simply just filled with hot air! This makes them a great cooking tool as they use air to heat food compared to traditional deep fryers that use oil to cook food. Air Fryers do not cook in the same way as deep fryers, they cook using much less oil meaning they are also less dirty than most deep fryers – making them extremely healthy.

Unlike the deep fat fryer, where food is submerged in hot oil, the Tower Air Fryer uses convention heat to circulate the hot air to cook the food which mimics the process that happens in a normal fan oven. This process relies on a chemical process known as the Maillard reaction that makes the exterior of the food crisp up giving you that extra tasty result!

Less of the science now and back to the practical bits… another really handy feature of the Tower Air Fryer is the built-in timer. This timer will automatically shut down the fryer when the timer reaches zero, meaning that you can keep your busy life on track whilst the air fryer does it's thing!

Five Features of Tower Air Fryers

There are so many great features of the Tower Air Fryer which makes it extremely difficult to define them down to just five! The first great feature we feel like we should mention is the lack of fat! By cooking with little to no oil means that the air fryer allows you to watch your waistline so simply. The technology of the Air Fryer means that you can cook all of your favourite meals the healthy way.

Another great feature of the Tower Air Fryer is the speed! The timer on the Air Fryer only goes up to 30 minutes, meaning that most meals can be cooked in this time or less. This is brilliant for the busy family on the go or the quick meal at the end of a long day in the office making for a

great grab and go meal.

Not only does the Tower Air Fryer help you to watch your waistline in record time, there's also so much choice! With over one hundred different cookbooks just for Air Fryer recipes there definitely is something for everyone. From a juicy steak without the wait to an outstanding fried chicken, the options are almost endless! But do not fear, if you are a vegetarian or fancy something on the light size, brussels sprouts and carrots can get a new lease of life with an extra level of crispness!

Save energy and reduce your utility bills by using the Tower Air Fryer. There has never been a better opportunity to reduce your energy usage to help not only your wallet but the environment too! You can save up to 50% on energy in the kitchen with Tower Air Fryers which can save you up to £210 per year on your energy bill – what's not to love!

The final feature that is almost too good to believe is the capacity. The Tower Air Fryer has an outstanding capacity of 2.2 litres. This means you are able to fit in a wide variety of foods at once from baby potatoes to steak to chicken drumsticks – you name it and I'm sure it would fit into the Tower Air Fryer!

Tower Air Fryer Cooking Tips

Before using your Tower Air Fryer for the first time be sure to remove all of the packaging and ensure that there is no damage to the cord or the Air Fryer itself. Thoroughly clean all parts of the Air Fryer paying close attention to the basket and pan using a simple solution of washing-up liquid and hot water.

Always ensure that the air fryer has been placed on a stable and heat-resistant surface. Make sure that your air fryer is placed away from other objects and surfaces to prevent them being damaged by the steam that is created from the air fryer.

Be sure to read through the settings guide that highlights specific instructions such as the minimum and maximum grams for each food type as well as the typical cooking times and temperatures.

Before using the Air Fryer for the first-time, it is always a good idea to give it a little test run! If your air fryer is a multi-function then it will have a preheat button. Once preheating is complete you will help a short simple beep which indicates that it has come up to temperature.

To make sure that your first batch of homemade fries are as crispy as possible make sure that the fries are completely dry before adding oil to them and placing the into the Air Fryer. You can also try to cut the potatoes themselves into thinner, smaller fries as well as adding slightly more oil in order to have a crispier result.

Never press the basket release button when removing the basket from the Tower Air Fryer. If you press the release button on the basket whilst carrying and transporting the basket it could fall and cause further accidents. Ensure to only press the basket release button when you're ready to greet your freshly made fries – always ensuring they have a stable, heat-resistant surface to be placed onto.

Don't panic if white smoke comes out of your Tower Air Fryer! This is normal if you are preparing greasy ingredients due to the large amount of oil that is in the food basket – this doesn't affect your appliance or the final result so definitely continue to cook up those greasy burgers.

Cleaning and Care

Always clean the appliance after every use by removing the mains plug from the wall socket to let the appliance cool down. You can also use degreasing liquid in order to remove any remaining dirt. Please note that the pan and basket are hand-wash only so do not place either of these parts of the appliance in the dishwasher.

If dirt or left over food is stuck within the basket or bottom of the pan, fill the pan up with hot water and a splash of washing-up liquid. Then allow this to soak for around ten to fifteen minutes to ensure that all dirt has been lifted.

Chapter 2 Snacks and Appetizers

Beef and Mango Skewers

Prep time: 10 minutes | Cook time: 4 to 7 minutes | Serves 4

340 g beef sirloin tip, cut into
1-inch cubes
2 tablespoons balsamic vinegar
1 tablespoon olive oil
1 tablespoon honey

½ teaspoon dried marjoram
Pinch of salt
Freshly ground black pepper, to
taste
1 mango

Preheat the air fryer to 200°C. Put the beef cubes in a medium bowl and add the balsamic vinegar, olive oil, honey, marjoram, salt, and pepper. Mix well, then massage the marinade into the beef with your hands. Set aside. To prepare the mango, stand it on end and cut the skin off, using a sharp knife. Then carefully cut around the oval pit to remove the flesh. Cut the mango into 1-inch cubes. Thread metal skewers alternating with three beef cubes and two mango cubes. Roast the skewers in the air fryer basket for 4 to 7 minutes, or until the beef is browned and at least 63°C. Serve hot.

Soft white cheese Stuffed Jalapeño Poppers

Prep time: 12 minutes | Cook time: 6 to 8 minutes | Serves 10

227 g soft white cheese, at
room temperature
240 ml panko breadcrumbs,
divided
2 tablespoons fresh parsley,

minced
1 teaspoon chilli powder
10 jalapeño peppers, halved and
seeded
Cooking oil spray

In a small bowl, whisk the soft white cheese, 120 ml of panko, the parsley, and chilli powder until combined. Stuff the cheese mixture into the jalapeño halves. Sprinkle the tops of the stuffed jalapeños with the remaining 120 ml of panko and press it lightly into the filling. Insert the crisper plate into the basket and the basket into the unit. Preheat the unit by selecting AIR FRY, setting the temperature to 192°C, and setting the time to 3 minutes. Select START/STOP to begin. Once the unit is preheated, spray the crisper plate with cooking oil. Place the poppers into the basket. Select AIR FRY, set the temperature to 192°C, and set the time to 8 minutes. Select START/STOP to begin. After 6 minutes, check the poppers. If they are softened and the cheese is melted, they are done. If not, resume cooking. When the cooking is complete, serve warm.

Pepperoni Pizza Dip

Prep time: 10 minutes | Cook time: 10 minutes | Serves 6

170 g soft white cheese
177 ml shredded Italian cheese
blend
60 ml sour cream
1½ teaspoons dried Italian
seasoning
¼ teaspoon garlic salt
¼ teaspoon onion powder
177 ml pizza sauce

120 ml sliced miniature
pepperoni
60 ml sliced black olives
1 tablespoon thinly sliced green
onion
Cut-up raw vegetables, toasted
baguette slices, pitta chips, or
tortilla chips, for serving

In a small bowl, combine the soft white cheese, 60 ml of the shredded cheese, the sour cream, Italian seasoning, garlic salt, and onion powder. Stir until smooth and the ingredients are well blended. Spread the mixture in a baking pan. Top with the pizza sauce, spreading to the edges. Sprinkle with the remaining 120 ml shredded cheese. Arrange the pepperoni slices on top of the cheese. Top with the black olives and green onion. Place the pan in the air fryer basket. Set the air fryer to 176°C for 10 minutes, or until the pepperoni is beginning to brown on the edges and the cheese is bubbly and lightly browned. Let stand for 5 minutes before serving with vegetables, toasted baguette slices, pitta chips, or tortilla chips.

Spicy Tortilla Chips

Prep time: 5 minutes | Cook time: 8 to 12 minutes | Serves 4

½ teaspoon ground cumin
½ teaspoon paprika
½ teaspoon chilli powder
½ teaspoon salt

Pinch cayenne pepper
8 (6-inch) corn tortillas, each
cut into 6 wedges
Cooking spray

Preheat the air fryer to 192°C. Lightly spritz the air fryer basket with cooking spray. Stir together the cumin, paprika, chilli powder, salt, and pepper in a small bowl. Working in batches, arrange the tortilla wedges in the air fryer basket in a single layer. Lightly mist them with cooking spray. Sprinkle some seasoning mixture on top of the tortilla wedges. Air fry for 4 to 6 minutes, shaking the basket halfway through, or until the chips are lightly browned and crunchy. Repeat with the remaining tortilla wedges and seasoning mixture. Let the tortilla chips cool for 5 minutes and serve.

Browned Ricotta with Capers and Lemon

Prep time: 10 minutes | Cook time: 8 to 10 minutes | Serves 4 to 6

355 ml whole milk ricotta cheese

2 tablespoons extra-virgin olive oil

2 tablespoons capers, rinsed

Zest of 1 lemon, plus more for garnish

1 teaspoon finely chopped fresh rosemary

Pinch crushed red pepper flakes

Salt and freshly ground black pepper, to taste

1 tablespoon grated Parmesan cheese

Preheat the air fryer to 192°C. In a mixing bowl, stir together the ricotta cheese, olive oil, capers, lemon zest, rosemary, red pepper flakes, salt, and pepper until well combined. Spread the mixture evenly in a baking dish and place it in the air fryer basket. Air fry for 8 to 10 minutes until the top is nicely browned. Remove from the basket and top with a sprinkle of grated Parmesan cheese. Garnish with the lemon zest and serve warm.

Authentic Scotch Eggs

Prep time: 15 minutes | Cook time: 11 to 13 minutes | Serves 6

680 g bulk lean chicken or turkey sausage

3 raw eggs, divided

355 ml dried breadcrumbs,

divided

120 ml plain flour

6 hardboiled eggs, peeled

Cooking oil spray

In a large bowl, combine the chicken sausage, 1 raw egg, and 120 ml of breadcrumbs and mix well. Divide the mixture into 6 pieces and flatten each into a long oval. In a shallow bowl, beat the remaining 2 raw eggs. Place the flour in a small bowl. Place the remaining 240 ml of breadcrumbs in a second small bowl. Roll each hardboiled egg in the flour and wrap one of the chicken sausage pieces around each egg to encircle it completely. One at a time, roll the encased eggs in the flour, dip in the beaten eggs, and finally dip in the breadcrumbs to coat. Insert the crisper plate into the basket and the basket into the unit. Preheat the unit by selecting AIR FRY, setting the temperature to 192°C, and setting the time to 3 minutes. Select START/STOP to begin. Once the unit is preheated, spray the crisper plate with cooking oil. Place the eggs in a single layer into the basket and spray them with oil. Select AIR FRY, set the temperature to 192°C, and set the time to 13 minutes. Select START/STOP to begin. 1After about 6 minutes, use tongs to turn the eggs and spray them with more oil. Resume cooking for 5 to 7 minutes more, or until the chicken is thoroughly cooked and the Scotch eggs are browned. 1When the cooking is complete, serve warm.

Bacon-Wrapped Pickle Spears

Prep time: 10 minutes | Cook time: 8 minutes | Serves 4

8 to 12 slices bacon

60 ml soft white cheese

60 ml shredded Mozzarella

cheese

8 dill pickle spears

120 ml ranch dressing

Lay the bacon slices on a flat surface. In a medium bowl, combine the soft white cheese and Mozzarella. Stir until well blended. Spread the cheese mixture over the bacon slices. Place a pickle spear on a bacon slice and roll the bacon around the pickle in a spiral, ensuring the pickle is fully covered. (You may need to use more than one slice of bacon per pickle to fully cover the spear.) Tuck in the ends to ensure the bacon stays put. Repeat to wrap all the pickles. Place the wrapped pickles in the air fryer basket in a single layer. Set the air fryer to 204°C for 8 minutes, or until the bacon is cooked through and crisp on the edges. Serve the pickle spears with ranch dressing on the side.

Shrimp Toasts with Sesame Seeds

Prep time: 15 minutes | Cook time: 6 to 8 minutes | Serves 4 to 6

230 g raw shrimp, peeled and deveined

1 egg, beaten

2 spring onions, chopped, plus more for garnish

2 tablespoons chopped fresh coriander

2 teaspoons grated fresh ginger

1 to 2 teaspoons sriracha sauce

1 teaspoon soy sauce

½ teaspoon toasted sesame oil

6 slices thinly sliced white sandwich bread

120 ml sesame seeds

Cooking spray

Thai chilli sauce, for serving

Preheat the air fryer to 204°C. Spritz the air fryer basket with cooking spray. In a food processor, add the shrimp, egg, spring onions, coriander, ginger, sriracha sauce, soy sauce and sesame oil, and pulse until chopped finely. You'll need to stop the food processor occasionally to scrape down the sides. Transfer the shrimp mixture to a bowl. On a clean work surface, cut the crusts off the sandwich bread. Using a brush, generously brush one side of each slice of bread with shrimp mixture. Place the sesame seeds on a plate. Press bread slices, shrimp-side down, into sesame seeds to coat evenly. Cut each slice diagonally into quarters. Spread the coated slices in a single layer in the air fryer basket. Air fry in batches for 6 to 8 minutes, or until golden and crispy. Flip the bread slices halfway through. Repeat with the remaining bread slices. Transfer to a plate and let cool for 5 minutes. Top with the chopped spring onions and serve warm with Thai chilli sauce.

Greens Chips with Curried Yoghurt Sauce

Prep time: 10 minutes | Cook time: 5 to 6 minutes | Serves 4

240 ml low-fat Greek yoghurt
1 tablespoon freshly squeezed lemon juice
1 tablespoon curry powder
½ bunch curly kale, stemmed, ribs removed and discarded,

leaves cut into 2- to 3-inch pieces
½ bunch chard, stemmed, ribs removed and discarded, leaves cut into 2- to 3-inch pieces
1½ teaspoons olive oil

In a small bowl, stir together the yoghurt, lemon juice, and curry powder. Set aside. In a large bowl, toss the kale and chard with the olive oil, working the oil into the leaves with your hands. This helps break up the fibres in the leaves so the chips are tender. Air fry the greens in batches at 200ºC for 5 to 6 minutes, until crisp, shaking the basket once during cooking. Serve with the yoghurt sauce.

Peppery Chicken Meatballs

Prep time: 5 minutes | Cook time: 13 to 20 minutes | Makes 16 meatballs

2 teaspoons olive oil
60 ml minced onion
60 ml minced red pepper
2 vanilla wafers, crushed

1 egg white
½ teaspoon dried thyme
230 g minced chicken breast

Preheat the air fryer to 188ºC. In a baking pan, mix the olive oil, onion, and red pepper. Put the pan in the air fryer. Air fry for 3 to 5 minutes, or until the vegetables are tender. In a medium bowl, mix the cooked vegetables, crushed wafers, egg white, and thyme until well combined Mix in the chicken, gently but thoroughly, until everything is combined. Form the mixture into 16 meatballs and place them in the air fryer basket. Air fry for 10 to 15 minutes, or until the meatballs reach an internal temperature of 74ºC on a meat thermometer. Serve immediately.

Caramelized Onion Dip with White Cheese

Prep time: 5 minutes | Cook time: 30 minutes | Serves 8 to 10

1 tablespoon butter
1 medium onion, halved and thinly sliced
¼ teaspoon rock salt, plus additional for seasoning
113 g soft white cheese
120 ml sour cream

¼ teaspoon onion powder
1 tablespoon chopped fresh chives
Black pepper, to taste
Thick-cut potato crisps or vegetable crisps

Place the butter in a baking pan. Place the pan in the air fryer basket. Set the air fryer to 92ºC for 1 minute, or until the butter is melted. Add the onions and salt to the pan. Set the air fryer to 92ºC for 15 minutes, or until onions are softened. Set the air fryer to 192ºC for 15 minutes, until onions are a deep golden brown, stirring two or three times during the cooking time. Let cool completely. In a medium bowl, stir together the cooked onions, soft white cheese, sour cream, onion powder, and chives. Season with salt and pepper. Cover and refrigerate for 2 hours to allow the flavours to blend. Serve the dip with potato crisps or vegetable crisps.

Crispy Filo Artichoke Triangles

Prep time: 15 minutes | Cook time: 9 to 12 minutes | Makes 18 triangles

60 ml Ricotta cheese
1 egg white
80 ml minced and drained artichoke hearts
3 tablespoons grated Mozzarella

cheese
½ teaspoon dried thyme
6 sheets frozen filo pastry, thawed
2 tablespoons melted butter

Preheat the air fryer to 204ºC. In a small bowl, combine the Ricotta cheese, egg white, artichoke hearts, Mozzarella cheese, and thyme, and mix well. Cover the filo pastry with a damp kitchen towel while you work so it doesn't dry out. Using one sheet at a time, place on the work surface and cut into thirds lengthwise. Put about 1½ teaspoons of the filling on each strip at the base. Fold the bottom right-hand tip of phyllo over the filling to meet the other side in a triangle, then continue folding in a triangle. Brush each triangle with butter to seal the edges. Repeat with the remaining phyllo dough and filling. Place the triangles in the air fryer basket. Bake, 6 at a time, for about 3 to 4 minutes, or until the filo is golden brown and crisp. Serve hot.

Goat Cheese and Garlic Crostini

Prep time: 3 minutes | Cook time: 5 minutes | Serves 4

1 wholemeal baguette
60 ml olive oil
2 garlic cloves, minced

113 g goat cheese
2 tablespoons fresh basil, minced

Preheat the air fryer to 192ºC. Cut the baguette into ½-inch-thick slices. In a small bowl, mix together the olive oil and garlic, then brush it over one side of each slice of bread. Place the olive-oil-coated bread in a single layer in the air fryer basket and bake for 5 minutes. Meanwhile, in a small bowl, mix together the goat cheese and basil. Remove the toast from the air fryer, then spread a thin layer of the goat cheese mixture over the top of each piece and serve.

Courgette Fries with Roasted Garlic Aioli

Prep time: 20 minutes | Cook time: 12 minutes |
Serves 4

1 tablespoon vegetable oil	Courgette Fries:
½ head green or savoy cabbage,	120 ml flour
finely shredded	2 eggs, beaten
Roasted Garlic Aioli:	240 ml seasoned breadcrumbs
1 teaspoon roasted garlic	Salt and pepper, to taste
120 ml mayonnaise	1 large courgette, cut into
2 tablespoons olive oil	½-inch sticks
Juice of ½ lemon	Olive oil
Salt and pepper, to taste	

Make the aioli: Combine the roasted garlic, mayonnaise, olive oil and lemon juice in a bowl and whisk well. Season the aioli with salt and pepper to taste. Prepare the courgette fries. Create a dredging station with three shallow dishes. Place the flour in the first shallow dish and season well with salt and freshly ground black pepper. Put the beaten eggs in the second shallow dish. In the third shallow dish, combine the breadcrumbs, salt and pepper. Dredge the courgette sticks, coating with flour first, then dipping them into the eggs to coat, and finally tossing in breadcrumbs. Shake the dish with the breadcrumbs and pat the crumbs onto the courgette sticks gently with your hands, so they stick evenly. Place the courgette fries on a flat surface and let them sit at least 10 minutes before air frying to let them dry out a little. Preheat the air fryer to 204°C. Spray the courgette sticks with olive oil and place them into the air fryer basket. You can air fry the courgette in two layers, placing the second layer in the opposite direction to the first. Air fry for 12 minutes turning and rotating the fries halfway through the cooking time. Spray with additional oil when you turn them over. Serve courgette fries warm with the roasted garlic aioli.

Vegetable Pot Stickers

Prep time: 12 minutes | Cook time: 11 to 18 minutes
| Makes 12 pot stickers

240 ml shredded red cabbage	2 garlic cloves, minced
60 ml chopped button	2 teaspoons grated fresh ginger
mushrooms	12 gyoza/pot sticker wrappers
60 ml grated carrot	2½ teaspoons olive oil, divided
2 tablespoons minced onion	

In a baking pan, combine the red cabbage, mushrooms, carrot, onion, garlic, and ginger. Add 1 tablespoon of water. Place in the air fryer and air fry at 188°C for 3 to 6 minutes, until the vegetables are crisp-tender. Drain and set aside. Working one at a time, place the pot sticker wrappers on a work surface. Top each wrapper with a scant 1 tablespoon of the filling. Fold half of the wrapper over the other half to form a half circle. Dab one edge with water and

press both edges together. To another pan, add 1¼ teaspoons of olive oil. Put half of the pot stickers, seam-side up, in the pan. Air fry for 5 minutes, or until the bottoms are light golden brown. Add 1 tablespoon of water and return the pan to the air fryer. Air fry for 4 to 6 minutes more, or until hot. Repeat with the remaining pot stickers, remaining 1¼ teaspoons of oil, and another tablespoon of water. Serve immediately.

Hush Puppies

Prep time: 45 minutes | Cook time: 10 minutes |
Serves 12

240 ml self-raising yellow	1 large egg
cornmeal	80 ml canned creamed corn
120 ml plain flour	240 ml minced onion
1 teaspoon sugar	2 teaspoons minced jalapeño
1 teaspoon salt	pepper
1 teaspoon freshly ground black	2 tablespoons olive oil, divided
pepper	

Thoroughly combine the cornmeal, flour, sugar, salt, and pepper in a large bowl. Whisk together the egg and corn in a small bowl. Pour the egg mixture into the bowl of cornmeal mixture and stir to combine. Stir in the minced onion and jalapeño. Cover the bowl with plastic wrap and place in the refrigerator for 30 minutes. Preheat the air fryer to 192°C. Line the air fryer basket with parchment paper and lightly brush it with 1 tablespoon of olive oil. Scoop out the cornmeal mixture and form into 24 balls, about 1 inch. Arrange the balls in the parchment paper-lined basket, leaving space between each ball. Air fry in batches for 5 minutes. Shake the basket and brush the balls with the remaining 1 tablespoon of olive oil. Continue cooking for 5 minutes until golden brown. Remove the balls (hush puppies) from the basket and serve on a plate.

Sea Salt Potato Crisps

Prep time: 30 minutes | Cook time: 27 minutes |
Serves 4

Oil, for spraying	1 tablespoon oil
4 medium yellow potatoes such	⅛ to ¼ teaspoon fine sea salt
as Maris Pipers	

Line the air fryer basket with parchment and spray lightly with oil. Using a mandoline or a very sharp knife, cut the potatoes into very thin slices. Place the slices in a bowl of cold water and let soak for about 20 minutes. Drain the potatoes, transfer them to a plate lined with paper towels, and pat dry. Drizzle the oil over the potatoes, sprinkle with the salt, and toss to combine. Transfer to the prepared basket. Air fry at 92°C for 20 minutes. Toss the crisps, increase the heat to 204°C, and cook for another 5 to 7 minutes, until crispy.

Baked Spanakopita Dip

Prep time: 10 minutes | Cook time: 15 minutes |
Serves 2

Olive oil cooking spray
3 tablespoons olive oil, divided
2 tablespoons minced white onion
2 garlic cloves, minced
1 L fresh spinach
113 g soft white cheese, softened

113 g feta cheese, divided
Zest of 1 lemon
¼ teaspoon ground nutmeg
1 teaspoon dried dill
½ teaspoon salt
Pitta chips, carrot sticks, or sliced bread for serving (optional)

Preheat the air fryer to 182°C. Coat the inside of a 6-inch ramekin or baking dish with olive oil cooking spray. In a large skillet over medium heat, heat 1 tablespoon of the olive oil. Add the onion, then cook for 1 minute. Add in the garlic and cook, stirring for 1 minute more. Reduce the heat to low and mix in the spinach and water. Let this cook for 2 to 3 minutes, or until the spinach has wilted. Remove the skillet from the heat. In a medium bowl, combine the soft white cheese, 57 g of the feta, and the remaining 2 tablespoons of olive oil, along with the lemon zest, nutmeg, dill, and salt. Mix until just combined. Add the vegetables to the cheese base and stir until combined. Pour the dip mixture into the prepared ramekin and top with the remaining 57 g of feta cheese. Place the dip into the air fryer basket and cook for 10 minutes, or until heated through and bubbling. Serve with pitta chips, carrot sticks, or sliced bread.

Shishito Peppers with Herb Dressing

Prep time: 10 minutes | Cook time: 6 minutes |
Serves 2 to 4

170 g shishito or Padron peppers
1 tablespoon vegetable oil
Rock salt and freshly ground black pepper, to taste
120 ml mayonnaise
2 tablespoons finely chopped fresh basil leaves
2 tablespoons finely chopped

fresh flat-leaf parsley
1 tablespoon finely chopped fresh tarragon
1 tablespoon finely chopped fresh chives
Finely grated zest of ½ lemon
1 tablespoon fresh lemon juice
Flaky sea salt, for serving

Preheat the air fryer to 204°C. In a bowl, toss together the shishitos and oil to evenly coat and season with rock salt and black pepper. Transfer to the air fryer and air fry for 6 minutes, shaking the basket halfway through, or until the shishitos are blistered and lightly charred. Meanwhile, in a small bowl, whisk together the mayonnaise, basil, parsley, tarragon, chives, lemon zest, and lemon juice. Pile the peppers on a plate, sprinkle with flaky sea salt, and serve hot with the dressing.

Rosemary-Garlic Shoestring Fries

Prep time: 5 minutes | Cook time: 18 minutes |
Serves 2

1 large russet or Maris Piper potato (about 340 g), scrubbed clean, and julienned
1 tablespoon vegetable oil
Leaves from 1 sprig fresh

rosemary
Rock salt and freshly ground black pepper, to taste
1 garlic clove, thinly sliced
Flaky sea salt, for serving

Preheat the air fryer to 204°C. Place the julienned potatoes in a large colander and rinse under cold running water until the water runs clear. Spread the potatoes out on a double-thick layer of paper towels and pat dry. In a large bowl, combine the potatoes, oil, and rosemary. Season with rock salt and pepper and toss to coat evenly. Place the potatoes in the air fryer and air fry for 18 minutes, shaking the basket every 5 minutes and adding the garlic in the last 5 minutes of cooking, or until the fries are golden brown and crisp. Transfer the fries to a plate and sprinkle with flaky sea salt while they're hot. Serve immediately.

Crispy Mozzarella Sticks

Prep time: 8 minutes | Cook time: 5 minutes | Serves 4

120 ml plain flour
1 egg, beaten
120 ml panko breadcrumbs
120 ml grated Parmesan cheese
1 teaspoon Italian seasoning

½ teaspoon garlic salt
6 Mozzarella sticks, halved crosswise
Olive oil spray

Put the flour in a small bowl. Put the beaten egg in another small bowl. In a medium bowl, stir together the panko, Parmesan cheese, Italian seasoning, and garlic salt. Roll a Mozzarella-stick half in the flour, dip it into the egg, and then roll it in the panko mixture to coat. Press the coating lightly to make sure the breadcrumbs stick to the cheese. Repeat with the remaining 11 Mozzarella sticks. Insert the crisper plate into the basket and the basket into the unit. Preheat the unit by selecting AIR FRY, setting the temperature to 204°C, and setting the time to 3 minutes. Select START/STOP to begin. Once the unit is preheated, spray the crisper plate with olive oil and place a parchment paper liner in the basket. Place the Mozzarella sticks into the basket and lightly spray them with olive oil. Select AIR FRY, set the temperature to 204°C, and set the time to 5 minutes. Select START/STOP to begin. When the cooking is complete, the Mozzarella sticks should be golden and crispy. Let the sticks stand for 1 minute before transferring them to a serving plate. Serve warm.

Jalapeño Poppers

Prep time: 10 minutes | Cook time: 20 minutes | Serves 4

Oil, for spraying
227 g soft white cheese
177 ml gluten-free breadcrumbs, divided
2 tablespoons chopped fresh
parsley
½ teaspoon granulated garlic
½ teaspoon salt
10 jalapeño peppers, halved and seeded

Line the air fryer basket with parchment and spray lightly with oil. In a medium bowl, mix together the soft white cheese, half of the breadcrumbs, the parsley, garlic, and salt. Spoon the mixture into the jalapeño halves. Gently press the stuffed jalapeños in the remaining breadcrumbs. Place the stuffed jalapeños in the prepared basket. Air fry at 188°C for 20 minutes, or until the cheese is melted and the breadcrumbs are crisp and golden brown.

Lemon-Pepper Chicken Drumsticks

Prep time: 30 minutes | Cook time: 30 minutes | Serves 2

2 teaspoons freshly ground coarse black pepper
1 teaspoon baking powder
½ teaspoon garlic powder
4 chicken drumsticks (113 g each)
Rock salt, to taste
1 lemon

In a small bowl, stir together the pepper, baking powder, and garlic powder. Place the drumsticks on a plate and sprinkle evenly with the baking powder mixture, turning the drumsticks so they're well coated. Let the drumsticks stand in the refrigerator for at least 1 hour or up to overnight. Sprinkle the drumsticks with salt, then transfer them to the air fryer, standing them bone-end up and leaning against the wall of the air fryer basket. Air fry at 192°C until cooked through and crisp on the outside, about 30 minutes. Transfer the drumsticks to a serving platter and finely grate the zest of the lemon over them while they're hot. Cut the lemon into wedges and serve with the warm drumsticks.

Lemony Pear Chips

Prep time: 15 minutes | Cook time: 9 to 13 minutes | Serves 4

2 firm Bosc or Anjou pears, cut crosswise into ⅛-inch-thick slices
1 tablespoon freshly squeezed
lemon juice
½ teaspoon ground cinnamon
⅛ teaspoon ground cardamom

Preheat the air fryer to 192°C. Separate the smaller stem-end pear rounds from the larger rounds with seeds. Remove the core and seeds from the larger slices. Sprinkle all slices with lemon juice, cinnamon, and cardamom. Put the smaller chips into the air fryer basket. Air fry for 3 to 5 minutes, or until light golden brown, shaking the basket once during cooking. Remove from the air fryer. Repeat with the larger slices, air frying for 6 to 8 minutes, or until light golden brown, shaking the basket once during cooking. Remove the chips from the air fryer. Cool and serve or store in an airtight container at room temperature up for to 2 days.

Skinny Fries

Prep time: 10 minutes | Cook time: 15 minutes per batch | Serves 2

2 to 3 russet or Maris Piper potatoes, peeled and cut into ¼-inch sticks
2 to 3 teaspoons olive or vegetable oil
Salt, to taste

Cut the potatoes into ¼-inch strips. (A mandolin with a julienne blade is really helpful here.) Rinse the potatoes with cold water several times and let them soak in cold water for at least 10 minutes or as long as overnight. Preheat the air fryer to 192°C. Drain and dry the potato sticks really well, using a clean kitchen towel. Toss the fries with the oil in a bowl and then air fry the fries in two batches at 192°C for 15 minutes, shaking the basket a couple of times while they cook. Add the first batch of French fries back into the air fryer basket with the finishing batch and let everything warm through for a few minutes. As soon as the fries are done, season them with salt and transfer to a plate or basket. Serve them warm with ketchup or your favourite dip.

Onion Pakoras

Prep time: 30 minutes | Cook time: 10 minutes per batch | Serves 2

2 medium brown or white onions, sliced (475 ml)
120 ml chopped fresh coriander
2 tablespoons vegetable oil
1 tablespoon chickpea flour
1 tablespoon rice flour, or 2
tablespoons chickpea flour
1 teaspoon ground turmeric
1 teaspoon cumin seeds
1 teaspoon rock salt
½ teaspoon cayenne pepper
Vegetable oil spray

In a large bowl, combine the onions, coriander, oil, chickpea flour, rice flour, turmeric, cumin seeds, salt, and cayenne. Stir to combine. Cover and let stand for 30 minutes or up to overnight. (This allows the onions to release moisture, creating a batter.) Mix well before using. Spray the air fryer basket generously with vegetable oil spray. Drop half of the batter in 6 heaping tablespoons into the basket. Set the air fryer to 176°C for 8 minutes. Carefully turn the pakoras over and spray with oil spray. Set the air fryer for 2 minutes, or until the batter is cooked through and crisp. Repeat with remaining batter to make 6 more pakoras, checking at 6 minutes for doneness. Serve hot.

Polenta Fries with Chilli-Lime Mayo

Prep time: 10 minutes | Cook time: 28 minutes | Serves 4

Polenta Fries:

2 teaspoons vegetable or olive oil

¼ teaspoon paprika

450 g prepared polenta, cut into 3-inch × ½-inch strips

Chilli-Lime Mayo:

120 ml mayonnaise

1 teaspoon chilli powder

1 teaspoon chopped fresh coriander

¼ teaspoon ground cumin

Juice of ½ lime

Salt and freshly ground black pepper, to taste

Preheat the air fryer to 204°C. Mix the oil and paprika in a bowl. Add the polenta strips and toss until evenly coated. Transfer the polenta strips to the air fry basket and air fry for 28 minutes until the fries are golden brown, shaking the basket once during cooking. Season as desired with salt and pepper. Meanwhile, whisk together all the ingredients for the chilli-lime mayo in a small bowl. Remove the polenta fries from the air fryer to a plate and serve alongside the chilli-lime mayo as a dipping sauce.

Chapter 3 Beans and Grains

Baked Mushroom-Barley Pilaf

Prep time: 5 minutes | Cook time: 37 minutes | Serves 4

Olive oil cooking spray	475 ml vegetable broth
2 tablespoons olive oil	1 tablespoon fresh thyme,
227 g button mushrooms, diced	chopped
½ brown onion, diced	½ teaspoon salt
2 garlic cloves, minced	¼ teaspoon smoked paprika
235 ml pearl barley	Fresh parsley, for garnish

Preheat the air fryer to 192°C. Lightly coat the inside of a 1.2 L capacity casserole dish with olive oil cooking spray. (The shape of the casserole dish will depend upon the size of the air fryer, but it needs to be able to hold at least 1.2 L.) In a large skillet, heat the olive oil over medium heat. Add the mushrooms and onion and cook, stirring occasionally, for 5 minutes, or until the mushrooms begin to brown. Add the garlic and cook for an additional 2 minutes. Transfer the vegetables to a large bowl. Add the barley, broth, thyme, salt, and paprika. Pour the barley-and-vegetable mixture into the prepared casserole dish and place the dish into the air fryer. Bake for 15 minutes. Stir the barley mixture. Reduce the heat to 182°C, then return the barley to the air fryer and bake for 15 minutes more. Remove from the air fryer and let sit for 5 minutes before fluffing with a fork and topping with fresh parsley.

Sweet Potato Black Bean Burgers

Prep time: 10 minutes | Cook time: 10 minutes | Serves 4

1 (425 g) can black beans, drained and rinsed	60 to 120 ml wholemeal breadcrumbs
235 ml mashed sweet potato	1 tablespoon olive oil
½ teaspoon dried oregano	For serving:
¼ teaspoon dried thyme	Wholemeal buns or wholemeal
¼ teaspoon dried marjoram	pittas
1 garlic clove, minced	Plain Greek yoghurt
¼ teaspoon salt	Avocado
¼ teaspoon black pepper	Lettuce
1 tablespoon lemon juice	Tomato
235 ml cooked brown rice	Red onion

Preheat the air fryer to 192°C. In a large bowl, use the back of a fork to mash the black beans until there are no large pieces left. Add the mashed sweet potato, oregano, thyme, marjoram, garlic, salt, pepper, and lemon juice, and mix until well combined. Stir in the cooked rice. Add in 60 ml wholemeal breadcrumbs and stir. Check to see if the mixture is dry enough to form patties. If it seems too wet and loose, add an additional 60 ml breadcrumbs and stir. Form the dough into 4 patties. Place them into the air fryer basket in a single layer, making sure that they don't touch each other. Brush half of the olive oil onto the patties and bake for 5 minutes. Flip the patties over, brush the other side with the remaining oil and bake for an additional 4 to 5 minutes. Serve on toasted wholemeal buns or wholemeal pittas with a spoonful of yoghurt and avocado, lettuce, tomato, and red onion as desired.

Spicy Lentil Patties

Prep time: 15 minutes | Cook time: 10 minutes | Serves 4

235 ml cooked brown lentils	½ teaspoon dried oregano
60 ml fresh parsley leaves	¼ teaspoon salt
120 ml shredded carrots	¼ teaspoon black pepper
¼ red onion, minced	120 ml wholemeal breadcrumbs
¼ red pepper, minced	For serving:
1 jalapeño, seeded and minced	Wholemeal buns or wholemeal
2 garlic cloves, minced	pittas
1 egg	Plain Greek yoghurt
2 tablespoons lemon juice	Tomato
2 tablespoons olive oil, divided	Lettuce
½ teaspoon onion powder	Red Onion
½ teaspoon smoked paprika	

Preheat the air fryer to 192°C. In a food processor, pulse the lentils and parsley mostly smooth. (You will want some bits of lentils in the mixture.) Pour the lentils into a large bowl, and combine with the carrots, onion, pepper, jalapeño, garlic, egg, lemon juice, and 1 tablespoon olive oil. Add the onion powder, paprika, oregano, salt, pepper, and breadcrumbs. Stir everything together until the seasonings and breadcrumbs are well distributed. Form the dough into 4 patties. Place them into the air fryer basket in a single layer, making sure that they don't touch each other. Brush the remaining 1 tablespoon of olive oil over the patties. Bake for 5 minutes. Flip the patties over and bake for an additional 5 minutes. Serve on toasted wholemeal buns or wholemeal pittas with a spoonful of yoghurt and lettuce, tomato, and red onion as desired.

Red Lentil and Goat Cheese Stuffed Tomatoes

Prep time: 10 minutes | Cook time: 15 minutes | Serves 4

4 tomatoes	¼ teaspoon salt
120 ml cooked red lentils	¼ teaspoon black pepper
1 garlic clove, minced	110 g goat cheese
1 tablespoon minced red onion	2 tablespoons shredded
4 basil leaves, minced	Parmesan cheese

Preheat the air fryer to 192°C. Slice the top off of each tomato. Using a knife and spoon, cut and scoop out half of the flesh inside of the tomato. Place it into a medium bowl. To the bowl with the tomato, add the cooked lentils, garlic, onion, basil, salt, pepper, and goat cheese. Stir until well combined. Spoon the filling into the scooped-out cavity of each of the tomatoes, then top each one with ½ tablespoon of shredded Parmesan cheese. Place the tomatoes in a single layer in the air fryer basket and bake for 15 minutes.

Herbed Green Lentil Rice Balls

Prep time: 5 minutes | Cook time: 11 minutes | Serves 6

120 ml cooked green lentils	235 ml cooked brown rice
2 garlic cloves, minced	1 tablespoon lemon juice
¼ white onion, minced	1 tablespoon olive oil
60 ml parsley leaves	½ teaspoon salt
5 basil leaves	

Preheat the air fryer to 192°C. In a food processor, pulse the cooked lentils with the garlic, onion, parsley, and basil until mostly smooth. (You will want some bits of lentils in the mixture.) Pour the lentil mixture into a large bowl, and stir in brown rice, lemon juice, olive oil, and salt. Stir until well combined. Form the rice mixture into 1-inch balls. Place the rice balls in a single layer in the air fryer basket, making sure that they don't touch each other. Fry for 6 minutes. Turn the rice balls and then fry for an additional 4 to 5 minutes, or until browned on all sides.

Roasted White Beans with Peppers

Prep time: 5 minutes | Cook time: 15 minutes | Serves 4

Olive oil cooking spray	3 garlic cloves, minced
2 (425 g) cans white beans, or	1 tablespoon olive oil
cannellini beans, drained and	¼ to ½ teaspoon salt
rinsed	½ teaspoon black pepper
1 red pepper, diced	1 rosemary sprig
½ red onion, diced	1 bay leaf

Preheat the air fryer to 182°C. Lightly coat the inside of a 1.2 L capacity casserole dish with olive oil cooking spray. (The shape of the casserole dish will depend upon the size of the air fryer, but it needs to be able to hold at least 1.2 L.) In a large bowl, combine the beans, red pepper, onion, garlic, olive oil, salt, and pepper. Pour the bean mixture into the prepared casserole dish, place the rosemary and bay leaf on top, and then place the casserole dish into the air fryer. Roast for 15 minutes. Remove the rosemary and bay leaves, then stir well before serving.

Savoury Gigantes Plaki (Baked Giant White Beans)

Prep time: 5 minutes | Cook time: 30 minutes | Serves 4

Olive oil cooking spray	2 garlic cloves, minced
1 (425 g) can cooked butter	½ brown onion, diced
beans, drained and rinsed	½ teaspoon salt
235 ml diced fresh tomatoes	60 ml olive oil
½ tablespoon tomato paste	60 ml fresh parsley, chopped

Preheat the air fryer to 192°C. Lightly coat the inside of a 1.2 L capacity casserole dish with olive oil cooking spray. (The shape of the casserole dish will depend upon the size of the air fryer, but it needs to be able to hold at least 1.2 L.) In a large bowl, combine the butter beans, tomatoes, tomato paste, garlic, onion, salt, and olive oil, mixing until all ingredients are combined. Pour the mixture into the prepared casserole dish and top with the chopped parsley. Bake in the air fryer for 15 minutes. Stir well, then return to the air fryer and bake for 15 minutes more.

Greek Baked Beans

Prep time: 5 minutes | Cook time: 30 minutes | Serves 4

Olive oil cooking spray	2 garlic cloves, minced
1 (425 g) can cannellini beans,	2 tablespoons chopped fresh
drained and rinsed	dill
1 (425 g) can butter beans,	½ teaspoon salt
drained and rinsed	½ teaspoon black pepper
½ brown onion, diced	1 bay leaf
1 (230 g) can tomato sauce	1 tablespoon balsamic vinegar
1½ tablespoons raw honey	60 g feta cheese, crumbled, for
60 ml olive oil	serving

Preheat the air fryer to 182°C. Lightly coat the inside of a 1.2 L capacity casserole dish with olive oil cooking spray. (The shape of the casserole dish will depend upon the size of the air fryer, but it needs to be able to hold at least 1.2 L.) In a large bowl, combine all ingredients except the feta cheese and stir until well combined. Pour the bean mixture into the prepared casserole dish. Bake in the air fryer for 30 minutes. Remove from the air fryer and remove and discard the bay leaf. Sprinkle crumbled feta over the top before serving.

Buckwheat Bake with Root Vegetables

Prep time: 15 minutes | Cook time: 30 minutes | Serves 6

Olive oil cooking spray	oil, divided
2 large potatoes, cubed	2 rosemary sprigs
2 carrots, sliced	235 ml buckwheat groats
1 small swede, cubed	475 ml vegetable broth
2 celery stalks, chopped	2 garlic cloves, minced
½ teaspoon smoked paprika	½ brown onion, chopped
60 ml plus 1 tablespoon olive	1 teaspoon salt

Preheat the air fryer to 192ºC. Lightly coat the inside of a 1.2 L capacity casserole dish with olive oil cooking spray. (The shape of the casserole dish will depend upon the size of the air fryer, but it needs to be able to hold at least 1.2 L.) In a large bowl, toss the potatoes, carrots, swede, and celery with the paprika and 60 ml olive oil. Pour the vegetable mixture into the prepared casserole dish and top with the rosemary sprigs. Place the casserole dish into the air fryer and bake for 15 minutes. While the vegetables are cooking, rinse and drain the buckwheat groats. In a medium saucepan over medium-high heat, combine the groats, vegetable broth, garlic, onion, and salt with the remaining 1 tablespoon olive oil. Bring the mixture to a boil, then reduce the heat to low, cover, and cook for 10 to 12 minutes. Remove the casserole dish from the air fryer. Remove the rosemary sprigs and discard. Pour the cooked buckwheat into the dish with the vegetables and stir to combine. Cover with aluminium foil and bake for an additional 15 minutes. Stir before serving.

Baked Farro Risotto with Sage

Prep time: 5 minutes | Cook time: 35 minutes | Serves 6

Olive oil cooking spray	1 tablespoon fresh sage,
350 ml uncooked farro, emmer	chopped
wheat or quinoa	½ teaspoon salt
600 ml chicken broth	2 tablespoons olive oil
235 ml tomato sauce	235 ml Parmesan cheese,
1 brown onion, diced	grated, divided
3 garlic cloves, minced	

Preheat the air fryer to 192ºC. Lightly coat the inside of a 1.2 L capacity casserole dish with olive oil cooking spray. (The shape of the casserole dish will depend upon the size of the air fryer, but it needs to be able to hold at least 1.2 L.) In a large bowl, combine the farro, broth, tomato sauce, onion, garlic, sage, salt, olive oil, and 120 ml of the Parmesan. Pour the farro mixture into the prepared casserole dish and cover with aluminium foil. Bake for 20 minutes, then uncover and stir. Sprinkle the remaining 120 ml Parmesan over the top and bake for 15 minutes more. Stir well before serving.

Mediterranean Creamed Green Peas

Prep time: 5 minutes | Cook time: 25 minutes | Serves 4

235 ml cauliflower florets, fresh	2 tablespoons fresh thyme
or frozen	leaves, chopped
½ white onion, roughly	1 teaspoon fresh rosemary
chopped	leaves, chopped
2 tablespoons olive oil	½ teaspoon salt
120 ml unsweetened almond	½ teaspoon black pepper
milk	Shredded Parmesan cheese, for
700 ml green peas, fresh or	garnish
frozen	Fresh parsley, for garnish
3 garlic cloves, minced	

Preheat the air fryer to 192ºC. In a large bowl, combine the cauliflower florets and onion with the olive oil and toss well to coat. Put the cauliflower-and-onion mixture into the air fryer basket in an even layer and bake for 15 minutes. Transfer the cauliflower and onion to a food processor. Add the almond milk and pulse until smooth. In a medium saucepan, combine the cauliflower purée, peas, garlic, thyme, rosemary, salt, and pepper and mix well. Cook over medium heat for an additional 10 minutes, stirring regularly. Serve with a sprinkle of Parmesan cheese and chopped fresh parsley.

Moroccan-Style Rice and Chickpea Bake

Prep time: 10 minutes | Cook time: 45 minutes | Serves 6

Olive oil cooking spray	½ teaspoon ground turmeric
235 ml long-grain brown rice	½ teaspoon ground ginger
535 ml chicken stock	½ teaspoon onion powder
1 (439 g) can chickpeas,	½ teaspoon salt
drained and rinsed	¼ teaspoon ground cinnamon
120 ml diced carrot	¼ teaspoon garlic powder
120 ml green peas	¼ teaspoon black pepper
1 teaspoon ground cumin	Fresh parsley, for garnish

Preheat the air fryer to 192ºC. Lightly coat the inside of a 1.2 L capacity casserole dish with olive oil cooking spray. (The shape of the casserole dish will depend upon the size of the air fryer, but it needs to be able to hold at least 1.2 L.) In the casserole dish, combine the rice, stock, chickpeas, carrot, peas, cumin, turmeric, ginger, onion powder, salt, cinnamon, garlic powder, and black pepper. Stir well to combine. Cover loosely with aluminium foil. Place the covered casserole dish into the air fryer and bake for 20 minutes. Remove from the air fryer and stir well. Place the casserole back into the air fryer, uncovered, and bake for 25 minutes more. Fluff with a spoon and sprinkle with fresh chopped parsley before serving.

Chapter 4 Breakfasts

Egg Tarts

Prep time: 10 minutes | Cook time: 17 to 20 minutes | Makes 2 tarts

⅓ sheet frozen puff pastry, thawed	2 eggs
Cooking oil spray	¼ teaspoon salt, divided
120 ml shredded Cheddar cheese	1 teaspoon minced fresh parsley (optional)

Insert the crisper plate into the basket and the basket into the unit. Preheat the unit by selecting BAKE, setting the temperature to 200ºC, and setting the time to 3 minutes. Select START/STOP to begin. Lay the puff pastry sheet on a piece of parchment paper and cut it in half. Once the unit is preheated, spray the crisper plate with cooking oil. Transfer the 2 squares of pastry to the basket, keeping them on the parchment paper. Select BAKE, set the temperature to 200ºC, and set the time to 20 minutes. Select START/STOP to begin. After 10 minutes, use a metal spoon to press down the center of each pastry square to make a well. Divide the cheese equally between the baked pastries. Carefully crack an egg on top of the cheese, and sprinkle each with the salt. Resume cooking for 7 to 10 minutes. When the cooking is complete, the eggs will be cooked through. Sprinkle each with parsley (if using) and serve.

Baked Potato Breakfast Boats

Prep time: 10 minutes | Cook time: 20 minutes | Serves 4

2 large white potatoes, scrubbed	2 tablespoons chopped, cooked bacon
Olive oil	
Salt and freshly ground black pepper, to taste	235 ml shredded Cheddar cheese
4 eggs	

Poke holes in the potatoes with a fork and microwave on full power for 5 minutes. Turn potatoes over and cook an additional 3 to 5 minutes, or until the potatoes are fork-tender. Cut the potatoes in half lengthwise and use a spoon to scoop out the inside of the potato. Be careful to leave a layer of potato so that it makes a sturdy "boat." Preheat the air fryer to 176ºC. Lightly spray the air fryer basket with olive oil. Spray the skin side of the potatoes with oil and sprinkle with salt and pepper to taste. Place the potato skins in the air fryer basket, skin-side down. Crack one egg into each potato skin. Sprinkle ½ tablespoon of bacon pieces and 60 ml shredded cheese on top of each egg. Sprinkle with salt and pepper to taste. Air fry until the yolk is slightly runny, 5 to 6 minutes, or until the yolk is fully cooked, 7 to 10 minutes.

Cauliflower Avocado Toast

Prep time: 15 minutes | Cook time: 8 minutes | Serves 2

1 (40 g) steamer bag cauliflower	1 ripe medium avocado
1 large egg	½ teaspoon garlic powder
120 ml shredded Mozzarella cheese	¼ teaspoon ground black pepper

Cook cauliflower according to package instructions. Remove from bag and place into cheesecloth or clean towel to remove excess moisture. Place cauliflower into a large bowl and mix in egg and Mozzarella. Cut a piece of parchment to fit your air fryer basket. Separate the cauliflower mixture into two, and place it on the parchment in two mounds. Press out the cauliflower mounds into a ¼-inch-thick rectangle. Place the parchment into the air fryer basket. Adjust the temperature to 204ºC and set the timer for 8 minutes. Flip the cauliflower halfway through the cooking time. When the timer beeps, remove the parchment and allow the cauliflower to cool 5 minutes. Cut open the avocado and remove the pit. Scoop out the inside, place it in a medium bowl, and mash it with garlic powder and pepper. Spread onto the cauliflower. Serve immediately.

Simple Scotch Eggs

Prep time: 5 minutes | Cook time: 25 minutes | Serves 4

4 large hard boiled eggs	8 slices thick-cut bacon
1 (340 g) package pork sausage meat	4 wooden toothpicks, soaked in water for at least 30 minutes

Slice the sausage meat into four parts and place each part into a large circle. Put an egg into each circle and wrap it in the sausage. Put in the refrigerator for 1 hour. Preheat the air fryer to 234ºC. Make a cross with two pieces of thick-cut bacon. Put a wrapped egg in the center, fold the bacon over top of the egg, and secure with a toothpick. Air fry in the preheated air fryer for 25 minutes. Serve immediately.

Canadian Bacon Muffin Sandwiches

Prep time: 5 minutes | Cook time: 8 minutes | Serves 4

4 English muffins, split	4 slices cheese
8 slices back bacon	Cooking spray

Preheat the air fryer to 188°C. Make the sandwiches: Top each of 4 muffin halves with 2 slices of bacon, 1 slice of cheese, and finish with the remaining muffin half. Put the sandwiches in the air fryer basket and spritz the tops with cooking spray. Bake for 4 minutes. Flip the sandwiches and bake for another 4 minutes. Divide the sandwiches among four plates and serve warm.

Parmesan Sausage Egg Muffins

Prep time: 5 minutes | Cook time: 20 minutes | Serves 4

170 g Italian-seasoned sausage, sliced	Salt and ground black pepper, to taste
6 eggs	85 g Parmesan cheese, grated
30 ml double cream	

Preheat the air fryer to 176°C. Grease a muffin pan. Put the sliced sausage in the muffin pan. Beat the eggs with the cream in a bowl and season with salt and pepper. Pour half of the mixture over the sausages in the pan. Sprinkle with cheese and the remaining egg mixture. Bake in the preheated air fryer for 20 minutes or until set. Serve immediately.

Homemade Toaster Pastries

Prep time: 10 minutes | Cook time: 11 minutes | Makes 6 pastries

Oil, for spraying	475 ml icing sugar
1 (425 g) package refrigerated piecrust	3 tablespoons milk
6 tablespoons jam or preserves of choice	1 to 2 tablespoons sprinkles of choice

Preheat the air fryer to 176°C. Line the air fryer basket with parchment and spray lightly with oil. Cut the piecrust into 12 rectangles, about 3 by 4 inches each. You will need to reroll the dough scraps to get 12 rectangles. Spread 1 tablespoon of jam in the center of 6 rectangles, leaving ¼ inch around the edges. Pour some water into a small bowl. Use your finger to moisten the edge of each rectangle. Top each rectangle with another and use your fingers to press around the edges. Using the tines of a fork, seal the edges of the dough and poke a few holes in the top of each one. Place the pastries in the prepared basket. Air fry for 11 minutes. Let cool completely. In a medium bowl, whisk together the icing sugar and milk. Spread the icing over the tops of the pastries and add sprinkles. Serve immediately.

Peppered Maple Bacon Knots

Prep time: 5 minutes | Cook time: 7 to 8 minutes | Serves 6

450 g maple smoked/cured bacon rashers	60 ml brown sugar
60 ml maple syrup	Coarsely cracked black peppercorns, to taste

Preheat the air fryer to 200°C. On a clean work surface, tie each bacon strip in a loose knot. Stir together the maple syrup and brown sugar in a bowl. Generously brush this mixture over the bacon knots. Working in batches, arrange the bacon knots in the air fryer basket. Sprinkle with the coarsely cracked black peppercorns. Air fry for 5 minutes. Flip the bacon knots and continue cooking for 2 to 3 minutes more, or until the bacon is crisp. Remove from the basket to a paper towel-lined plate. Repeat with the remaining bacon knots. Let the bacon knots cool for a few minutes and serve warm.

Sirloin Steaks with Eggs

Prep time: 8 minutes | Cook time: 14 minutes per batch | Serves 4

Cooking oil spray	1 teaspoon freshly ground black pepper, divided
4 (110 g) sirloin steaks	
1 teaspoon granulated garlic, divided	4 eggs
1 teaspoon salt, divided	½ teaspoon paprika

Insert the crisper plate into the basket and the basket into the unit. Preheat the unit by selecting AIR FRY, setting the temperature to 182°C, and setting the time to 3 minutes. Select START/STOP to begin. Once the unit is preheated, spray the crisper plate with cooking oil. Place 2 steaks into the basket; do not oil or season them at this time. Select AIR FRY, set the temperature to 182°C, and set the time to 9 minutes. Select START/STOP to begin. After 5 minutes, open the unit and flip the steaks. Sprinkle each with ¼ teaspoon of granulated garlic, ¼ teaspoon of salt, and ¼ teaspoon of pepper. Resume cooking until the steaks register at least 64°C on a food thermometer. When the cooking is complete, transfer the steaks to a plate and tent with aluminum foil to keep warm. Repeat steps 2, 3, and 4 with the remaining steaks. Spray 4 ramekins with olive oil. Crack 1 egg into each ramekin. Sprinkle the eggs with the paprika and remaining ½ teaspoon each of salt and pepper. Working in batches, place 2 ramekins into the basket. Select BAKE, set the temperature to 166°C, and set the time to 5 minutes. Select START/STOP to begin. When the cooking is complete and the eggs are cooked to 72°C, remove the ramekins and repeat step 7 with the remaining 2 ramekins. Serve the eggs with the steaks.

Sausage and Cheese Balls

Prep time: 10 minutes | Cook time: 12 minutes | Makes 16 balls

450 g pork sausage meat, removed from casings
120 ml shredded Cheddar cheese

30 g full-fat cream cheese, softened
1 large egg

Mix all ingredients in a large bowl. Form into sixteen (1-inch) balls. Place the balls into the air fryer basket. Adjust the temperature to 204°C and air fry for 12 minutes. Shake the basket two or three times during cooking. Sausage balls will be browned on the outside and have an internal temperature of at least 64°C when completely cooked. Serve warm.

Hearty Cheddar Biscuits

Prep time: 10 minutes | Cook time: 22 minutes | Makes 8 biscuits

550 ml self-raising flour
2 tablespoons sugar
120 ml butter, frozen for 15 minutes
120 ml grated Cheddar cheese,

plus more to melt on top
315 ml buttermilk
235 ml plain flour, for shaping
1 tablespoon butter, melted

Line a buttered 7-inch metal cake pan with parchment paper or a silicone liner. Combine the flour and sugar in a large mixing bowl. Grate the butter into the flour. Add the grated cheese and stir to coat the cheese and butter with flour. Then add the buttermilk and stir just until you can no longer see streaks of flour. The dough should be quite wet. Spread the plain (not self-raising) flour out on a small cookie sheet. With a spoon, scoop 8 evenly sized balls of dough into the flour, making sure they don't touch each other. With floured hands, coat each dough ball with flour and toss them gently from hand to hand to shake off any excess flour. Put each floured dough ball into the prepared pan, right up next to the other. This will help the biscuits rise, rather than spreading out. Preheat the air fryer to 192°C. Transfer the cake pan to the basket of the air fryer. Let the ends of the aluminum foil sling hang across the cake pan before returning the basket to the air fryer. Air fry for 20 minutes. Check the biscuits twice to make sure they are not getting too brown on top. If they are, re-arrange the aluminum foil strips to cover any brown parts. After 20 minutes, check the biscuits by inserting a toothpick into the center of the biscuits. It should come out clean. If it needs a little more time, continue to air fry for two extra minutes. Brush the tops of the biscuits with some melted butter and sprinkle a little more grated cheese on top if desired. Pop the basket back into the air fryer for another 2 minutes. Remove the cake pan from the air fryer. Let the biscuits cool for just a minute or two and then turn them out onto a plate and pull apart. Serve immediately.

Apple Cider Doughnut Holes

Prep time: 10 minutes | Cook time: 6 minutes | Makes 10 mini doughnuts

Doughnut Holes:
350 ml plain flour
2 tablespoons granulated sugar
2 teaspoons baking powder
1 teaspoon baking soda
½ teaspoon coarse or flaky salt
Pinch of freshly grated nutmeg
60 ml plus 2 tablespoons buttermilk, chilled
2 tablespoons apple cider or

apple juice, chilled
1 large egg, lightly beaten
Vegetable oil, for brushing
Glaze:
120 ml icing sugar
2 tablespoons unsweetened applesauce
¼ teaspoon vanilla extract
Pinch of coarse or flaky salt

Make the doughnut holes: In a bowl, whisk together the flour, granulated sugar, baking powder, baking soda, salt, and nutmeg until smooth. Add the buttermilk, cider, and egg and stir with a small rubber spatula or spoon until the dough just comes together. Using a 28 g ice cream scoop or 2 tablespoons, scoop and drop 10 balls of dough into the air fryer basket, spaced evenly apart, and brush the tops lightly with oil. Air fry at 176°C until the doughnut holes are golden brown and fluffy, about 6 minutes. Transfer the doughnut holes to a wire rack to cool completely. Make the glaze: In a small bowl, stir together the powdered sugar, applesauce, vanilla, and salt until smooth. Dip the tops of the doughnuts holes in the glaze, then let stand until the glaze sets before serving. If you're impatient and want warm doughnuts, have the glaze ready to go while the doughnuts cook, then use the glaze as a dipping sauce for the warm doughnuts, fresh out of the air fryer.

Spinach and Swiss Frittata with Mushrooms

Prep time: 10 minutes | Cook time: 20 minutes | Serves 4

Olive oil cooking spray
8 large eggs
½ teaspoon salt
½ teaspoon black pepper
1 garlic clove, minced
475 ml fresh baby spinach

110 g baby mushrooms, sliced
1 shallot, diced
120 ml shredded Swiss cheese, divided
Hot sauce, for serving (optional)

Preheat the air fryer to 182°C. Lightly coat the inside of a 6-inch round cake pan with olive oil cooking spray. In a large bowl, beat the eggs, salt, pepper, and garlic for 1 to 2 minutes, or until well combined. Fold in the spinach, mushrooms, shallot, and 60 ml the Swiss cheese. Pour the egg mixture into the prepared cake pan, and sprinkle the remaining 60 ml Swiss over the top. Place into the air fryer and bake for 18 to 20 minutes, or until the eggs are set in the center. Remove from the air fryer and allow to cool for 5 minutes. Drizzle with hot sauce (if using) before serving.

Breakfast Pitta

Prep time: 5 minutes | Cook time: 6 minutes | Serves 2

1 wholemeal pitta	¼ teaspoon dried oregano
2 teaspoons olive oil	¼ teaspoon dried thyme
½ shallot, diced	⅛ teaspoon salt
¼ teaspoon garlic, minced	2 tablespoons shredded
1 large egg	Parmesan cheese

Preheat the air fryer to 192°C. Brush the top of the pitta with olive oil, then spread the diced shallot and minced garlic over the pitta. Crack the egg into a small bowl or ramekin, and season it with oregano, thyme, and salt. Place the pitta into the air fryer basket, and gently pour the egg onto the top of the pitta. Sprinkle with cheese over the top. Bake for 6 minutes. Allow to cool for 5 minutes before cutting into pieces for serving.

BLT Breakfast Wrap

Prep time: 5 minutes | Cook time: 10 minutes | Serves 4

230 g reduced-salt bacon	4 plum tomatoes, sliced
8 tablespoons mayonnaise	Salt and freshly ground black
8 large romaine lettuce leaves	pepper, to taste

Arrange the bacon in a single layer in the air fryer basket. (It's OK if the bacon sits a bit on the sides.) Set the air fryer to 176°C and air fry for 10 minutes. Check for crispiness and air fry for 2 to 3 minutes longer if needed. Cook in batches, if necessary, and drain the grease in between batches. Spread 1 tablespoon of mayonnaise on each of the lettuce leaves and top with the tomatoes and cooked bacon. Season to taste with salt and freshly ground black pepper. Roll the lettuce leaves as you would a burrito, securing with a toothpick if desired.

Easy Buttermilk Biscuits

Prep time: 5 minutes | Cook time: 18 minutes |
Makes 16 biscuits

600 ml plain flour	½ teaspoon baking soda
1 tablespoon baking powder	8 tablespoons (1 stick) unsalted
1 teaspoon coarse or flaky salt	butter, at room temperature
1 teaspoon sugar	235 ml buttermilk, chilled

Stir together the flour, baking powder, salt, sugar, and baking powder in a large bowl. Add the butter and stir to mix well. Pour in the buttermilk and stir with a rubber spatula just until incorporated. Place the dough onto a lightly floured surface and roll the dough out to a disk, ½ inch thick. Cut out the biscuits with a 2-inch round cutter and re-roll any scraps until you have 16 biscuits. Preheat the air fryer to 164°C. Working in batches, arrange the biscuits in the air fryer basket in a single layer. Bake for about 18 minutes until the biscuits are golden brown. Remove from the basket to a plate and repeat with the remaining biscuits. Serve hot.

Mississippi Spice Muffins

Prep time: 15 minutes | Cook time: 13 minutes |
Makes 12 muffins

1 L plain flour	temperature
1 tablespoon ground cinnamon	475 ml sugar
2 teaspoons baking soda	2 large eggs, lightly beaten
2 teaspoons allspice	475 ml unsweetened applesauce
1 teaspoon ground cloves	60 ml chopped pecans
1 teaspoon salt	1 to 2 tablespoons oil
235 ml (2 sticks) butter, room	

In a large bowl, whisk the flour, cinnamon, baking soda, allspice, cloves, and salt until blended. In another large bowl, combine the butter and sugar. Using an electric mixer, beat the mixture for 2 to 3 minutes until light and fluffy. Add the beaten eggs and stir until blended. Add the flour mixture and applesauce, alternating between the two and blending after each addition. Stir in the pecans. Preheat the air fryer to 164°C. Spritz 12 silicone muffin cups with oil. Pour the batter into the prepared muffin cups, filling each halfway. Place the muffins in the air fryer basket. Air fry for 6 minutes. Shake the basket and air fry for 7 minutes more. The muffins are done when a toothpick inserted into the middle comes out clean.

Banana-Nut Muffins

Prep time: 5 minutes | Cook time: 15 minutes |
Makes 10 muffins

Oil, for spraying	1 large egg
2 very ripe bananas	1 teaspoon vanilla extract
120 ml packed light brown sugar	180 ml plain flour
80 ml rapeseed oil or vegetable oil	1 teaspoon baking powder
	1 teaspoon ground cinnamon
	120 ml chopped walnuts

Preheat the air fryer to 160°C. Spray 10 silicone muffin cups lightly with oil. In a medium bowl, mash the bananas. Add the brown sugar, rapeseed oil, egg, and vanilla and stir to combine. Fold in the flour, baking powder, and cinnamon until just combined. Add the walnuts and fold a few times to distribute throughout the batter. Divide the batter equally among the prepared muffin cups and place them in the basket. You may need to work in batches, depending on the size of your air fryer. Cook for 15 minutes, or until golden brown and a toothpick inserted into the center of a muffin comes out clean. The air fryer tends to brown muffins more than the oven, so don't be alarmed if they are darker than you're used to. They will still taste great. Let cool on a wire rack before serving.

Cheddar Soufflés

Prep time: 15 minutes | Cook time: 12 minutes | Serves 4

3 large eggs, whites and yolks separated

¼ teaspoon cream of tartar

120 ml shredded sharp Cheddar cheese

85 g cream cheese, softened

In a large bowl, beat egg whites together with cream of tartar until soft peaks form, about 2 minutes. In a separate medium bowl, beat egg yolks, Cheddar, and cream cheese together until frothy, about 1 minute. Add egg yolk mixture to whites, gently folding until combined. Pour mixture evenly into four ramekins greased with cooking spray. Place ramekins into air fryer basket. Adjust the temperature to 176°C and bake for 12 minutes. Eggs will be browned on the top and firm in the center when done. Serve warm.

Baked Peach Oatmeal

Prep time: 5 minutes | Cook time: 30 minutes | Serves 6

Olive oil cooking spray

475 ml certified gluten-free rolled oats

475 ml unsweetened almond milk

60 ml honey, plus more for drizzling (optional)

120 ml non-fat plain Greek yoghurt

1 teaspoon vanilla extract

½ teaspoon ground cinnamon

¼ teaspoon salt

350 ml diced peaches, divided, plus more for serving (optional)

Preheat the air fryer to 192°C. Lightly coat the inside of a 6-inch cake pan with olive oil cooking spray. In a large bowl, mix together the oats, almond milk, honey, yoghurt, vanilla, cinnamon, and salt until well combined. Fold in 180 ml peaches and then pour the mixture into the prepared cake pan. Sprinkle the remaining peaches across the top of the oatmeal mixture. Bake in the air fryer for 30 minutes. Allow to set and cool for 5 minutes before serving with additional fresh fruit and honey for drizzling, if desired.

Breakfast Sausage and Cauliflower

Prep time: 5 minutes | Cook time: 45 minutes | Serves 4

450 g sausage meat, cooked and crumbled

475 ml double/whipping cream

1 head cauliflower, chopped

235 ml grated Cheddar cheese,

plus more for topping

8 eggs, beaten

Salt and ground black pepper, to taste

Preheat the air fryer to 176°C. In a large bowl, mix the sausage, cream, chopped cauliflower, cheese and eggs. Sprinkle with salt and ground black pepper. Pour the mixture into a greased casserole dish. Bake in the preheated air fryer for 45 minutes or until firm. Top with more Cheddar cheese and serve.

Mexican Breakfast Pepper Rings

Prep time: 5 minutes | Cook time: 10 minutes | Serves 4

Olive oil

1 large red, yellow, or orange pepper, cut into four ¾-inch rings

4 eggs

Salt and freshly ground black pepper, to taste

2 teaspoons salsa

Preheat the air fryer to 176°C. Lightly spray a baking pan with olive oil. Place 2 bell pepper rings on the pan. Crack one egg into each bell pepper ring. Season with salt and black pepper. Spoon ½ teaspoon of salsa on top of each egg. Place the pan in the air fryer basket. Air fry until the yolk is slightly runny, 5 to 6 minutes or until the yolk is fully cooked, 8 to 10 minutes. Repeat with the remaining 2 pepper rings. Serve hot.

Simple Cinnamon Toasts

Prep time: 5 minutes | Cook time: 4 minutes | Serves 4

1 tablespoon salted butter

2 teaspoons ground cinnamon

4 tablespoons sugar

½ teaspoon vanilla extract

10 bread slices

Preheat the air fryer to 192°C. In a bowl, combine the butter, cinnamon, sugar, and vanilla extract. Spread onto the slices of bread. Put the bread inside the air fryer and bake for 4 minutes or until golden brown. Serve warm.

Meritage Eggs

Prep time: 5 minutes | Cook time: 8 minutes | Serves 2

2 teaspoons unsalted butter (or coconut oil for dairy-free), for greasing the ramekins

4 large eggs

2 teaspoons chopped fresh thyme

½ teaspoon fine sea salt

¼ teaspoon ground black pepper

2 tablespoons double cream (or unsweetened, unflavoured almond milk for dairy-free)

3 tablespoons finely grated Parmesan cheese (or chive cream cheese style spread, softened, for dairy-free)

Fresh thyme leaves, for garnish (optional)

Preheat the air fryer to 204°C. Grease two (110 g) ramekins with the butter. Crack 2 eggs into each ramekin and divide the thyme, salt, and pepper between the ramekins. Pour 1 tablespoon of the heavy cream into each ramekin. Sprinkle each ramekin with 1½ tablespoons of the Parmesan cheese. Place the ramekins in the air fryer and bake for 8 minutes for soft-cooked yolks (longer if you desire a harder yolk). Garnish with a sprinkle of ground black pepper and thyme leaves, if desired. Best served fresh.

Scotch Eggs

Prep time: 10 minutes | Cook time: 20 to 25 minutes | Serves 4

2 tablespoons flour, plus extra for coating	1 tablespoon water
450 g sausage meat	Oil for misting or cooking spray
4 hard-boiled eggs, peeled	Crumb Coating:
1 raw egg	180 ml panko bread crumbs
	180 ml flour

Combine flour with sausage meat and mix thoroughly. Divide into 4 equal portions and mold each around a hard-boiled egg so the sausage completely covers the egg. In a small bowl, beat together the raw egg and water. Dip sausage-covered eggs in the remaining flour, then the egg mixture, then roll in the crumb coating. Air fry at 182°C for 10 minutes. Spray eggs, turn, and spray other side. Continue cooking for another 10 to 15 minutes or until sausage is well done.

Double-Dipped Mini Cinnamon Biscuits

Prep time: 15 minutes | Cook time: 13 minutes | Makes 8 biscuits

475 ml blanched almond flour	1 large egg
120 ml liquid or powdered sweetener	1 teaspoon vanilla extract
1 teaspoon baking powder	3 teaspoons ground cinnamon
½ teaspoon fine sea salt	Glaze:
60 ml plus 2 tablespoons (¾ stick) very cold unsalted butter	120 ml powdered sweetener
60 ml unsweetened, unflavoured almond milk	60 ml double cream or unsweetened, unflavoured almond milk

Preheat the air fryer to 176°C. Line a pie pan that fits into your air fryer with parchment paper. In a medium-sized bowl, mix together the almond flour, sweetener (if powdered; do not add liquid sweetener), baking powder, and salt. Cut the butter into ½-inch squares, then use a hand mixer to work the butter into the dry ingredients. When you are done, the mixture should still have chunks of butter. In a small bowl, whisk together the almond milk, egg, and vanilla extract (if using liquid sweetener, add it as well) until blended. Using a fork, stir the wet ingredients into the dry ingredients until large clumps form. Add the cinnamon and use your hands to swirl it into the dough. Form the dough into sixteen 1-inch balls and place them on the prepared pan, spacing them about ½ inch apart. (If you're using a smaller air fryer, work in batches if necessary.) Bake in the air fryer until golden, 10 to 13 minutes. Remove from the air fryer and let cool on the pan for at least 5 minutes. While the biscuits bake, make the glaze: Place the powdered sweetener in a small bowl and slowly stir in the heavy cream with a fork. When the biscuits have cooled somewhat, dip the tops into the glaze, allow it to dry a bit, and then dip again for a thick glaze. Serve warm or at room temperature. Store unglazed biscuits in an airtight container in the refrigerator for up to 3 days or in the freezer for up to a month. Reheat in a preheated 176°C air fryer for 5 minutes, or until warmed through, and dip in the glaze as instructed above.

Poached Eggs on Whole Grain Avocado Toast

Prep time: 5 minutes | Cook time: 7 minutes | Serves 4

Olive oil cooking spray	4 pieces wholegrain bread
4 large eggs	1 avocado
Salt	Red pepper flakes (optional)
Black pepper	

Preheat the air fryer to 160°C. Lightly coat the inside of four small oven-safe ramekins with olive oil cooking spray. Crack one egg into each ramekin, and season with salt and black pepper. Place the ramekins into the air fryer basket. Close and set the timer to 7 minutes. While the eggs are cooking, toast the bread in a toaster. Slice the avocado in half lengthwise, remove the pit, and scoop the flesh into a small bowl. Season with salt, black pepper, and red pepper flakes, if desired. Using a fork, smash the avocado lightly. Spread a quarter of the smashed avocado evenly over each slice of toast. Remove the eggs from the air fryer, and gently spoon one onto each slice of avocado toast before serving.

Buffalo Chicken Breakfast Muffins

Prep time: 7 minutes | Cook time: 13 to 16 minutes | Serves 10

170 g shredded cooked chicken	1 teaspoon minced garlic
85 g blue cheese, crumbled	6 large eggs
2 tablespoons unsalted butter, melted	Sea salt and freshly ground black pepper, to taste
80 ml Buffalo hot sauce, such as Frank's RedHot	Avocado oil spray

In a large bowl, stir together the chicken, blue cheese, melted butter, hot sauce, and garlic. In a medium bowl or large liquid measuring cup, beat the eggs. Season with salt and pepper. Spray 10 silicone muffin cups with oil. Divide the chicken mixture among the cups, and pour the egg mixture over top. Place the cups in the air fryer and set to 150°C. Bake for 13 to 16 minutes, until the muffins are set and cooked through. (Depending on the size of your air fryer, you may need to cook the muffins in batches.)

Veggie Frittata

Prep time: 7 minutes | Cook time: 21 to 23 minutes | Serves 2

Avocado oil spray
60 ml diced red onion
60 ml diced red pepper
60 ml finely chopped broccoli
4 large eggs

85 g shredded sharp Cheddar cheese, divided
½ teaspoon dried thyme
Sea salt and freshly ground black pepper, to taste

Spray a pan well with oil. Put the onion, pepper, and broccoli in the pan, place the pan in the air fryer, and set to 176°C. Bake for 5 minutes. While the vegetables cook, beat the eggs in a medium bowl. Stir in half of the cheese, and season with the thyme, salt, and pepper. Add the eggs to the pan and top with the remaining cheese. Set the air fryer to 176°C. Bake for 16 to 18 minutes, until cooked through.

Asparagus and Bell Pepper Strata

Prep time: 10 minutes | Cook time: 14 to 20 minutes | Serves 4

8 large asparagus spears, trimmed and cut into 2-inch pieces
80 ml shredded carrot
120 ml chopped red pepper
2 slices wholemeal bread, cut

into ½-inch cubes
3 egg whites
1 egg
3 tablespoons 1% milk
½ teaspoon dried thyme

In a baking pan, combine the asparagus, carrot, red bell pepper, and 1 tablespoon of water. Bake in the air fryer at 166°C for 3 to 5 minutes, or until crisp-tender. Drain well. Add the bread cubes to the vegetables and gently toss. In a medium bowl, whisk the egg whites, egg, milk, and thyme until frothy. Pour the egg mixture into the pan. Bake for 11 to 15 minutes, or until the strata is slightly puffy and set and the top starts to brown. Serve.

Homemade Cherry Breakfast Tarts

Prep time: 15 minutes | Cook time: 20 minutes | Serves 6

Tarts:
2 refrigerated piecrusts
80 ml cherry preserves
1 teaspoon cornflour
Cooking oil

Frosting:
120 ml vanilla yoghurt
30 g cream cheese
1 teaspoon stevia
Rainbow sprinkles

Make the Tarts Place the piecrusts on a flat surface. Using a knife or pizza cutter, cut each piecrust into 3 rectangles, for 6 total. (I discard the unused dough left from slicing the edges.) In a small bowl, combine the preserves and cornflour. Mix well. Scoop 1 tablespoon of the preserves mixture onto the top half of each piece of piecrust. Fold the bottom of each piece up to close the tart. Using the back of a fork, press along the edges of each tart to seal. Spray the breakfast tarts with cooking oil and place them in the air fryer. I do not recommend stacking the breakfast tarts. They will stick together if stacked. You may need to prepare them in two batches. Bake at 375°F for 10 minutes. Allow the breakfast tarts to cool fully before removing from the air fryer. If necessary, repeat steps 5 and 6 for the remaining breakfast tarts. Make the Frosting In a small bowl, combine the yoghurt, cream cheese, and stevia. Mix well. Spread the breakfast tarts with frosting and top with sprinkles, and serve.

Egg in a Hole

Prep time: 5 minutes | Cook time: 5 minutes | Serves 1

1 slice bread
1 teaspoon butter, softened
1 egg
Salt and pepper, to taste

1 tablespoon shredded Cheddar cheese
2 teaspoons diced ham

Preheat the air fryer to 166°C. Place a baking dish in the air fryer basket. On a flat work surface, cut a hole in the center of the bread slice with a 2½-inch-diameter biscuit cutter. Spread the butter evenly on each side of the bread slice and transfer to the baking dish. Crack the egg into the hole and season as desired with salt and pepper. Scatter the shredded cheese and diced ham on top. Bake in the preheated air fryer for 5 minutes until the bread is lightly browned and the egg is cooked to your preference. Remove from the basket and serve hot.

French Toast Sticks

Prep time: 10 minutes | Cook time: 9 minutes | Serves 4

Oil, for spraying
6 large eggs
315 ml milk
2 teaspoons vanilla extract

1 teaspoon ground cinnamon
8 slices bread, cut into thirds
Syrup of choice, for serving

Preheat the air fryer to 188°C. Line the air fryer basket with parchment and spray lightly with oil. In a shallow bowl, whisk the eggs, milk, vanilla, and cinnamon. Dunk one piece of bread in the egg mixture, making sure to coat both sides. Work quickly so the bread doesn't get soggy. Immediately transfer the bread to the prepared basket. Repeat with the remaining bread, making sure the pieces don't touch each other. You may need to work in batches, depending on the size of your air fryer. Air fry for 5 minutes, flip, and cook for another 3 to 4 minutes, until browned and crispy. Serve immediately with your favorite syrup.

Bacon-and-Eggs Avocado

Prep time: 5 minutes | Cook time: 17 minutes | Serves 1

1 large egg	Fresh parsley, for serving
1 avocado, halved, peeled, and	(optional)
pitted	Sea salt flakes, for garnish
2 slices bacon	(optional)

Spray the air fryer basket with avocado oil. Preheat the air fryer to 160°C. Fill a small bowl with cool water. Soft-boil the egg: Place the egg in the air fryer basket. Air fry for 6 minutes for a soft yolk or 7 minutes for a cooked yolk. Transfer the egg to the bowl of cool water and let sit for 2 minutes. Peel and set aside. Use a spoon to carve out extra space in the center of the avocado halves until the cavities are big enough to fit the soft-boiled egg. Place the soft-boiled egg in the center of one half of the avocado and replace the other half of the avocado on top, so the avocado appears whole on the outside. Starting at one end of the avocado, wrap the bacon around the avocado to completely cover it. Use toothpicks to hold the bacon in place. Place the bacon-wrapped avocado in the air fryer basket and air fry for 5 minutes. Flip the avocado over and air fry for another 5 minutes, or until the bacon is cooked to your liking. Serve on a bed of fresh parsley, if desired, and sprinkle with salt flakes, if desired. Best served fresh. Store extras in an airtight container in the fridge for up to 4 days. Reheat in a preheated 160°C air fryer for 4 minutes, or until heated through.

Maple Granola

Prep time: 5 minutes | Cook time: 40 minutes |
Makes 475 ml

235 ml rolled oats	sunflower
3 tablespoons pure maple syrup	¼ teaspoon sea salt
1 tablespoon sugar	¼ teaspoon ground cinnamon
1 tablespoon neutral-flavored	¼ teaspoon vanilla extract
oil, such as refined coconut or	

Insert the crisper plate into the basket and the basket into the unit. Preheat the unit by selecting BAKE, setting the temperature to 120°C, and setting the time to 3 minutes. Select START/STOP to begin. In a medium bowl, stir together the oats, maple syrup, sugar, oil, salt, cinnamon, and vanilla until thoroughly combined. Transfer the granola to a 6-by-2-inch round baking pan. Once the unit is preheated, place the pan into the basket. Select BAKE, set the temperature to 120°C and set the time to 40 minutes. Select START/STOP to begin. After 10 minutes, stir the granola well. Resume cooking, stirring the granola every 10 minutes, for a total of 40 minutes, or until the granola is lightly browned and mostly dry. When the cooking is complete, place the granola on a plate to cool. It will become crisp as it cools. Store the completely cooled granola in an airtight container in a cool, dry place for 1 to 2 weeks.

Sausage and Egg Breakfast Burrito

Prep time: 5 minutes | Cook time: 30 minutes | Serves 6

6 eggs	(removed from casings)
Salt and pepper, to taste	120 ml salsa
Cooking oil	6 medium (8-inch) flour tortillas
120 ml chopped red pepper	120 ml shredded Cheddar
120 ml chopped green pepper	cheese
230 g chicken sausage meat	

In a medium bowl, whisk the eggs. Add salt and pepper to taste. Place a skillet on medium-high heat. Spray with cooking oil. Add the eggs. Scramble for 2 to 3 minutes, until the eggs are fluffy. Remove the eggs from the skillet and set aside. If needed, spray the skillet with more oil. Add the chopped red and green bell peppers. Cook for 2 to 3 minutes, until the peppers are soft. Add the sausage meat to the skillet. Break the sausage into smaller pieces using a spatula or spoon. Cook for 3 to 4 minutes, until the sausage is brown. Add the salsa and scrambled eggs. Stir to combine. Remove the skillet from heat. Spoon the mixture evenly onto the tortillas. To form the burritos, fold the sides of each tortilla in toward the middle and then roll up from the bottom. You can secure each burrito with a toothpick. Or you can moisten the outside edge of the tortilla with a small amount of water. I prefer to use a cooking brush, but you can also dab with your fingers. Spray the burritos with cooking oil and place them in the air fryer. Do not stack. Cook the burritos in batches if they do not all fit in the basket. Air fry at 204°C for 8 minutes. Open the air fryer and flip the burritos. Cook for an additional 2 minutes or until crisp. 1If necessary, repeat steps 8 and 9 for the remaining burritos. 1Sprinkle the Cheddar cheese over the burritos. Cool before serving.

Gluten-Free Granola Cereal

Prep time: 7 minutes | Cook time: 30 minutes |
Makes 820 ml

Oil, for spraying	1 tablespoon toasted sesame oil
350 ml gluten-free rolled oats	or vegetable oil
120 ml chopped walnuts	1 teaspoon ground cinnamon
120 ml chopped almonds	½ teaspoon salt
120 ml pumpkin seeds	120 ml dried cranberries
60 ml maple syrup or honey	

Preheat the air fryer to 120°C. Line the air fryer basket with parchment and spray lightly with oil. (Do not skip the step of lining the basket; the parchment will keep the granola from falling through the holes.) In a large bowl, mix together the oats, walnuts, almonds, pumpkin seeds, maple syrup, sesame oil, cinnamon, and salt. Spread the mixture in an even layer in the prepared basket. Cook for 30 minutes, stirring every 10 minutes. Transfer the granola to a bowl, add the dried cranberries, and toss to combine. Let cool to room temperature before storing in an airtight container.

Pitta and Pepperoni Pizza

Prep time: 10 minutes | Cook time: 6 minutes | Serves 1

1 teaspoon olive oil

1 tablespoon pizza sauce

1 pitta bread

6 pepperoni slices

60 ml grated Mozzarella cheese

¼ teaspoon garlic powder

¼ teaspoon dried oregano

Preheat the air fryer to 176°C. Grease the air fryer basket with olive oil. Spread the pizza sauce on top of the pitta bread. Put the pepperoni slices over the sauce, followed by the Mozzarella cheese. Season with garlic powder and oregano. Put the pitta pizza inside the air fryer and place a trivet on top. Bake in the preheated air fryer for 6 minutes and serve.

Tomato and Mozzarella Bruschetta

Prep time: 5 minutes | Cook time: 4 minutes | Serves 1

6 small loaf slices

120 ml tomatoes, finely chopped

85 g Mozzarella cheese, grated

1 tablespoon fresh basil, chopped

1 tablespoon olive oil

Preheat the air fryer to 176°C. Put the loaf slices inside the air fryer and air fry for about 3 minutes. Add the tomato, Mozzarella, basil, and olive oil on top. Air fry for an additional minute before serving.

Chapter 5 Family Favorites

Beignets

Prep time: 30 minutes | Cook time: 6 minutes | Makes 9 beignets

Oil, for greasing and spraying
700 ml plain flour, plus more for dusting
1½ teaspoons salt
1 (2¼-teaspoon) active dry yeast

235 ml milk
2 tablespoons packed light brown sugar
1 tablespoon unsalted butter
1 large egg
235 ml icing sugar

Oil a large bowl. In a small bowl, mix together the flour, salt, and yeast. Set aside. Pour the milk into a glass measuring cup and microwave in 1-minute intervals until it boils. In a large bowl, mix together the brown sugar and butter. Pour in the hot milk and whisk until the sugar has dissolved. Let cool to room temperature. Whisk the egg into the cooled milk mixture and fold in the flour mixture until a dough forms. On a lightly floured work surface, knead the dough for 3 to 5 minutes. Place the dough in the oiled bowl and cover with a clean kitchen towel. Let rise in a warm place for about 1 hour, or until doubled in size. Roll the dough out on a lightly floured work surface until it's about ¼ inch thick. Cut the dough into 3-inch squares and place them on a lightly floured baking sheet. Cover loosely with a kitchen towel and let rise again until doubled in size, about 30 minutes. Line the air fryer basket with parchment and spray lightly with oil. Place the dough squares in the prepared basket and spray lightly with oil. You may need to work in batches, depending on the size of your air fryer. Air fry at 200°C for 3 minutes, flip, spray with oil, and cook for another 3 minutes, until crispy. Dust with the icing sugar before serving.

Chinese-Inspired Spareribs

Prep time: 30 minutes | Cook time: 8 minutes | Serves 4

Oil, for spraying
340 g boneless pork spareribs, cut into 3-inch-long pieces
235 ml soy sauce
180 ml sugar
120 ml beef or chicken stock

60 ml honey
2 tablespoons minced garlic
1 teaspoon ground ginger
2 drops red food colouring (optional)

Line the air fryer basket with parchment and spray lightly with oil. Combine the ribs, soy sauce, sugar, beef stock, honey, garlic, ginger, and food colouring (if using) in a large zip-top plastic bag, seal, and shake well until completely coated. Refrigerate for at least

30 minutes. Place the ribs in the prepared basket. Air fry at 192°C for 8 minutes, or until the internal temperature reaches 74°C.

Old Bay Tilapia

Prep time: 15 minutes | Cook time: 6 minutes | Serves 4

Oil, for spraying
235 ml panko breadcrumbs
2 tablespoons Old Bay or all-purpose seasoning
2 teaspoons granulated garlic
1 teaspoon onion powder

½ teaspoon salt
¼ teaspoon freshly ground black pepper
1 large egg
4 tilapia fillets

Preheat the air fryer to 204°C. Line the air fryer basket with parchment and spray lightly with oil. In a shallow bowl, mix together the breadcrumbs, seasoning, garlic, onion powder, salt, and black pepper. In a small bowl, whisk the egg. Coat the tilapia in the egg, then dredge in the bread crumb mixture until completely coated. Place the tilapia in the prepared basket. You may need to work in batches, depending on the size of your air fryer. Spray lightly with oil. Cook for 4 to 6 minutes, depending on the thickness of the fillets, until the internal temperature reaches 64°C. Serve immediately.

Cajun Shrimp

Prep time: 15 minutes | Cook time: 9 minutes | Serves 4

Oil, for spraying
450 g jumbo raw shrimp, peeled and deveined
1 tablespoon Cajun seasoning
170 g cooked kielbasa, cut into thick slices
½ medium courgette, cut into ¼-inch-thick slices

½ medium yellow squash or butternut squash, cut into ¼-inch-thick slices
1 green pepper, seeded and cut into 1-inch pieces
2 tablespoons olive oil
½ teaspoon salt

Preheat the air fryer to 204°C. Line the air fryer basket with parchment and spray lightly with oil. In a large bowl, toss together the shrimp and Cajun seasoning. Add the kielbasa, courgette, squash, pepper, olive oil, and salt and mix well. Transfer the mixture to the prepared basket, taking care not to overcrowd. You may need to work in batches, depending on the size of your air fryer. Cook for 9 minutes, shaking and stirring every 3 minutes. Serve immediately.

Mixed Berry Crumble

Prep time: 10 minutes | Cook time: 11 to 16 minutes | Serves 4

120 ml chopped fresh strawberries	1 tablespoon honey
120 ml fresh blueberries	160 ml wholemeal pastry flour
80 ml frozen raspberries	3 tablespoons packed brown sugar
1 tablespoon freshly squeezed lemon juice	2 tablespoons unsalted butter, melted

In a baking pan, combine the strawberries, blueberries, and raspberries. Drizzle with the lemon juice and honey. In a small bowl, mix the pastry flour and brown sugar. Stir in the butter and mix until crumbly. Sprinkle this mixture over the fruit. Bake at 192°C for 11 to 16 minutes, or until the fruit is tender and bubbly and the topping is golden brown. Serve warm.

Scallops with Green Vegetables

Prep time: 15 minutes | Cook time: 8 to 11 minutes | Serves 4

235 ml green beans	½ teaspoon dried basil
235 ml frozen peas	½ teaspoon dried oregano
235 ml frozen chopped broccoli	340 g sea scallops
2 teaspoons olive oil	

In a large bowl, toss the green beans, peas, and broccoli with the olive oil. Place in the air fryer basket. Air fry at 204°C for 4 to 6 minutes, or until the vegetables are crisp-tender. Remove the vegetables from the air fryer basket and sprinkle with the herbs. Set aside. In the air fryer basket, put the scallops and air fry for 4 to 5 minutes, or until the scallops are firm and reach an internal temperature of just 64°C on a meat thermometer. Toss scallops with the vegetables and serve immediately.

Pork Stuffing Meatballs

Prep time: 10 minutes | Cook time: 12 minutes | Makes 35 meatballs

Oil, for spraying	1 tablespoon dried thyme
680 g minced pork	1 teaspoon salt
235 ml breadcrumbs	1 teaspoon freshly ground black pepper
120 ml milk	
60 ml minced onion	1 teaspoon finely chopped fresh parsley
1 large egg	
1 tablespoon dried rosemary	

Line the air fryer basket with parchment and spray lightly with oil. In a large bowl, mix together the minced pork, breadcrumbs, milk, onion, egg, rosemary, thyme, salt, black pepper, and parsley. Roll about 2 tablespoons of the mixture into a ball. Repeat with the rest of the mixture. You should have 30 to 35 meatballs. Place the meatballs in the prepared basket in a single layer, leaving space between each one. You may need to work in batches, depending on the size of your air fryer. Air fry at 200°C for 10 to 12 minutes, flipping after 5 minutes, or until golden brown and the internal temperature reaches 72°C.

Churro Bites

Prep time: 5 minutes | Cook time: 6 minutes | Makes 36 bites

Oil, for spraying	1 tablespoon ground cinnamon
1 (500 g) package frozen puffed pastry, thawed	120 ml icing sugar
	1 tablespoon milk
235 ml granulated sugar	

Preheat the air fryer to 204°C. Line the air fryer basket with parchment and spray lightly with oil. Unfold the puff pastry onto a clean work surface. Using a sharp knife, cut the dough into 36 bite-size pieces. Place the dough pieces in one layer in the prepared basket, taking care not to let the pieces touch or overlap. Cook for 3 minutes, flip, and cook for another 3 minutes, or until puffed and golden. In a small bowl, mix together the granulated sugar and cinnamon. In another small bowl, whisk together the icing sugar and milk. Dredge the bites in the cinnamon-sugar mixture until evenly coated. Serve with the icing on the side for dipping.

Veggie Tuna Melts

Prep time: 15 minutes | Cook time: 7 to 11 minutes | Serves 4

2 low-salt wholemeal English muffins, split	green parts, sliced
	80 ml fat-free Greek yoghurt
1 (170 g) can chunk light low-salt tuna, drained	2 tablespoons low-salt wholegrain mustard
235 ml shredded carrot	2 slices low-salt low-fat Swiss cheese, halved
80 ml chopped mushrooms	
2 spring onions, white and	

Place the English muffin halves in the air fryer basket. Air fry at 172°C for 3 to 4 minutes, or until crisp. Remove from the basket and set aside. In a medium bowl, thoroughly mix the tuna, carrot, mushrooms, spring onions, yoghurt, and mustard. Top each half of the muffins with one-fourth of the tuna mixture and a half slice of Swiss cheese. Air fry for 4 to 7 minutes, or until the tuna mixture is hot and the cheese melts and starts to brown. Serve immediately.

Berry Cheesecake

Prep time: 5 minutes | Cook time: 10 minutes | Serves 4

Oil, for spraying
227 g soft white cheese
6 tablespoons sugar
1 tablespoon sour cream

1 large egg
½ teaspoon vanilla extract
¼ teaspoon lemon juice
120 ml fresh mixed berries

Preheat the air fryer to 176°C. Line the air fryer basket with parchment and spray lightly with oil. In a blender, combine the soft white cheese, sugar, sour cream, egg, vanilla, and lemon juice and blend until smooth. Pour the mixture into a 4-inch springform pan. Place the pan in the prepared basket. Cook for 8 to 10 minutes, or until only the very centre jiggles slightly when the pan is moved. Refrigerate the cheesecake in the pan for at least 2 hours. Release the sides from the springform pan, top the cheesecake with the mixed berries, and serve.

Beef Jerky

Prep time: 30 minutes | Cook time: 2 hours | Serves 8

Oil, for spraying
450 g silverside steak, cut into thin, short slices
60 ml soy sauce
3 tablespoons packed light

brown sugar
1 tablespoon minced garlic
1 teaspoon ground ginger
1 tablespoon water

Line the air fryer basket with parchment and spray lightly with oil. Place the steak, soy sauce, brown sugar, garlic, ginger, and water in a zip-top plastic bag, seal, and shake well until evenly coated. Refrigerate for 30 minutes. Place the steak in the prepared basket in a single layer. You may need to work in batches, depending on the size of your air fryer. Air fry at 82°C for at least 2 hours. Add more time if you like your jerky a bit tougher.

Bacon-Wrapped Hot Dogs

Prep time: 5 minutes | Cook time: 10 minutes | Serves 4

Oil, for spraying
4 bacon slices
4 beef hot dogs

4 hot dog buns
Toppings of choice

Line the air fryer basket with parchment and spray lightly with oil. Wrap a strip of bacon tightly around each hot dog, taking care to cover the tips so they don't get too crispy. Secure with a toothpick at each end to keep the bacon from shrinking. Place the hot dogs in the prepared basket. Air fry at 192°C for 8 to 9 minutes, depending on how crispy you like the bacon. For extra-crispy, cook the hot dogs at 204°C for 6 to 8 minutes. Place the hot dogs in the buns, return them to the air fryer, and cook for another 1 to 2 minutes, or until the buns are warm. Add your desired toppings and serve.

Pecan Rolls

Prep time: 20 minutes | Cook time: 20 to 24 minutes | Makes 12 rolls

475 ml plain flour, plus more for dusting
2 tablespoons granulated sugar, plus 60 ml, divided
1 teaspoon salt
3 tablespoons butter, at room temperature

180 ml milk, whole or semi-skimmed
60 ml packed light brown sugar
120 ml chopped pecans, toasted
1 to 2 tablespoons oil
60 ml icing sugar (optional)

In a large bowl, whisk the flour, 2 tablespoons granulated sugar, and salt until blended. Stir in the butter and milk briefly until a sticky dough forms. In a small bowl, stir together the brown sugar and remaining 60 ml granulated sugar. Place a piece of parchment paper on a work surface and dust it with flour. Roll the dough on the prepared surface to ¼ inch thickness. Spread the sugar mixture over the dough. Sprinkle the pecans on top. Roll up the dough jelly roll-style, pinching the ends to seal. Cut the dough into 12 rolls. Preheat the air fryer to 160°C. Line the air fryer basket with parchment paper and spritz the parchment with oil. Place 6 rolls on the prepared parchment. Bake for 5 minutes. Flip the rolls and bake for 5 to 7 minutes more until lightly browned. Repeat with the remaining rolls. Sprinkle with icing sugar (if using).

Apple Pie Egg Rolls

Prep time: 10 minutes | Cook time: 8 minutes | Makes 6 rolls

Oil, for spraying
1 (600 g) can apple pie filling
1 tablespoon plain flour
½ teaspoon lemon juice

¼ teaspoon ground nutmeg
¼ teaspoon ground cinnamon
6 egg roll wrappers

Preheat the air fryer to 204°C. Line the air fryer basket with parchment and spray lightly with oil. In a medium bowl, mix together the pie filling, flour, lemon juice, nutmeg, and cinnamon. Lay out the egg roll wrappers on a work surface and spoon a dollop of pie filling in the centre of each. Fill a small bowl with water. Dip your finger in the water and, working one at a time, moisten the edges of the wrappers. Fold the wrapper like an envelope: First fold one corner into the centre. Fold each side corner in, and then fold over the remaining corner, making sure each corner overlaps a bit and the moistened edges stay closed. Use additional water and your fingers to seal any open edges. Place the rolls in the prepared basket and spray liberally with oil. You may need to work in batches, depending on the size of your air fryer. Cook for 4 minutes, flip, spray with oil, and cook for another 4 minutes, or until crispy and golden brown. Serve immediately.

Steak and Vegetable Kebabs

Prep time: 15 minutes | Cook time: 5 to 7 minutes | Serves 4

2 tablespoons balsamic vinegar	340 g silverside steak, cut into
2 teaspoons olive oil	1-inch pieces
½ teaspoon dried marjoram	1 red pepper, sliced
⅛ teaspoon freshly ground	16 button mushrooms
black pepper	235 ml cherry tomatoes

In a medium bowl, stir together the balsamic vinegar, olive oil, marjoram, and black pepper. Add the steak and stir to coat. Let stand for 10 minutes at room temperature. Alternating items, thread the beef, red pepper, mushrooms, and tomatoes onto 8 bamboo or metal skewers that fit in the air fryer. Air fry at 200°C for 5 to 7 minutes, or until the beef is browned and reaches at least 64°C on a meat thermometer. Serve immediately.

Cheesy Roasted Sweet Potatoes

Prep time: 7 minutes | Cook time: 18 to 23 minutes | Serves 4

2 large sweet potatoes, peeled	vinegar
and sliced	1 teaspoon dried thyme
1 teaspoon olive oil	60 ml grated Parmesan cheese
1 tablespoon white balsamic	

In a large bowl, drizzle the sweet potato slices with the olive oil and toss. Sprinkle with the balsamic vinegar and thyme and toss again. Sprinkle the potatoes with the Parmesan cheese and toss to coat. Roast the slices, in batches, in the air fryer basket at 204°C for 18 to 23 minutes, tossing the sweet potato slices in the basket once during cooking, until tender. Repeat with the remaining sweet potato slices. Serve immediately.

Filo Vegetable Triangles

Prep time: 15 minutes | Cook time: 6 to 11 minutes | Serves 6

3 tablespoons minced onion	2 tablespoons fat-free soft white
2 garlic cloves, minced	cheese, at room temperature
2 tablespoons grated carrot	6 sheets frozen filo pastry,
1 teaspoon olive oil	thawed
3 tablespoons frozen baby peas,	Olive oil spray, for coating the
thawed	dough

In a baking pan, combine the onion, garlic, carrot, and olive oil. Air fry at 200°C for 2 to 4 minutes, or until the vegetables are crisp-tender. Transfer to a bowl. Stir in the peas and soft white cheese to the vegetable mixture. Let cool while you prepare the dough. Lay one sheet of filo on a work surface and lightly spray with olive oil spray. Top with another sheet of filo. Repeat with the remaining 4 filo sheets; you'll have 3 stacks with 2 layers each. Cut each stack lengthwise into 4 strips (12 strips total). Place a scant 2 teaspoons of the filling near the bottom of each strip. Bring one corner up over the filling to make a triangle; continue folding the triangles over, as you would fold a flag. Seal the edge with a bit of water. Repeat with the remaining strips and filling. Air fry the triangles, in 2 batches, for 4 to 7 minutes, or until golden brown. Serve.

Meringue Cookies

Prep time: 15 minutes | Cook time: 1 hour 30 minutes | Makes 20 cookies

Oil, for spraying	235 ml sugar
4 large egg whites	Pinch cream of tartar

Preheat the air fryer to 60°C. Line the air fryer basket with parchment and spray lightly with oil. In a small heatproof bowl, whisk together the egg whites and sugar. Fill a small saucepan halfway with water, place it over medium heat, and bring to a light simmer. Place the bowl with the egg whites on the saucepan, making sure the bottom of the bowl does not touch the water. Whisk the mixture until the sugar is dissolved. Transfer the mixture to a large bowl and add the cream of tartar. Using an electric mixer, beat the mixture on high until it is glossy and stiff peaks form. Transfer the mixture to a piping bag or a zip-top plastic bag with a corner cut off. Pipe rounds into the prepared basket. You may need to work in batches, depending on the size of your air fryer. Cook for 1 hour 30 minutes. Turn off the air fryer and let the meringues cool completely inside. The residual heat will continue to dry them out.

Fish and Vegetable Tacos

Prep time: 15 minutes | Cook time: 9 to 12 minutes | Serves 4

450 g white fish fillets, such as	1 large carrot, grated
sole or cod	120 ml low-salt salsa
2 teaspoons olive oil	80 ml low-fat Greek yoghurt
3 tablespoons freshly squeezed	4 soft low-salt wholemeal
lemon juice, divided	tortillas
350 ml chopped red cabbage	

Brush the fish with the olive oil and sprinkle with 1 tablespoon of lemon juice. Air fry in the air fryer basket at 200°C for 9 to 12 minutes, or until the fish just flakes when tested with a fork. Meanwhile, in a medium bowl, stir together the remaining 2 tablespoons of lemon juice, the red cabbage, carrot, salsa, and yoghurt. When the fish is cooked, remove it from the air fryer basket and break it up into large pieces. Offer the fish, tortillas, and the cabbage mixture, and let each person assemble a taco.

Coconut Chicken Tenders

Prep time: 10 minutes | Cook time: 12 minutes | Serves 4

Oil, for spraying	180 ml panko breadcrumbs
2 large eggs	1 teaspoon salt
60 ml milk	½ teaspoon freshly ground
1 tablespoon hot sauce	black pepper
350 ml sweetened flaked or	450 g chicken tenders
desiccated coconut	

Line the air fryer basket with parchment and spray lightly with oil. In a small bowl, whisk together the eggs, milk, and hot sauce. In a shallow dish, mix together the coconut, breadcrumbs, salt, and black pepper. Coat the chicken in the egg mix, then dredge in the coconut mixture until evenly coated. Place the chicken in the prepared basket and spray liberally with oil. Air fry at 204°C for 6 minutes, flip, spray with more oil, and cook for another 6 minutes, or until the internal temperature reaches 74°C.

Steak Tips and Potatoes

Prep time: 10 minutes | Cook time: 20 minutes | Serves 4

Oil, for spraying	1 teaspoon Worcestershire
227 g baby gold potatoes, cut in	sauce
half	1 teaspoon granulated garlic
½ teaspoon salt	½ teaspoon salt
450 g steak, cut into ½-inch	½ teaspoon freshly ground
pieces	black pepper

Line the air fryer basket with parchment and spray lightly with oil. In a microwave-safe bowl, combine the potatoes and salt, then pour in about ½ inch of water. Microwave for 7 minutes, or until the potatoes are nearly tender. Drain. In a large bowl, gently mix together the steak, potatoes, Worcestershire sauce, garlic, salt, and black pepper. Spread the mixture in an even layer in the prepared basket. Air fry at 204°C for 12 to 17 minutes, stirring after 5 to 6 minutes. The cooking time will depend on the thickness of the meat and preferred doneness.

Fried Green Tomatoes

Prep time: 15 minutes | Cook time: 6 to 8 minutes | Serves 4

4 medium green tomatoes	120 ml panko breadcrumbs
80 ml plain flour	2 teaspoons olive oil
2 egg whites	1 teaspoon paprika
60 ml almond milk	1 clove garlic, minced
235 ml ground almonds	

Rinse the tomatoes and pat dry. Cut the tomatoes into ½-inch slices, discarding the thinner ends. Put the flour on a plate. In a shallow bowl, beat the egg whites with the almond milk until frothy. And on another plate, combine the almonds, breadcrumbs, olive oil, paprika, and garlic and mix well. Dip the tomato slices into the flour, then into the egg white mixture, then into the almond mixture to coat. Place four of the coated tomato slices in the air fryer basket. Air fry at 204°C for 6 to 8 minutes or until the tomato coating is crisp and golden brown. Repeat with remaining tomato slices and serve immediately.

Avocado and Egg Burrito

Prep time: 10 minutes | Cook time: 3 to 5 minutes | Serves 4

2 hard-boiled egg whites,	plus additional for serving
chopped	(optional)
1 hard-boiled egg, chopped	1 (34 g) slice low-salt, low-
1 avocado, peeled, pitted, and	fat processed cheese, torn into
chopped	pieces
1 red pepper, chopped	4 low-salt wholemeal flour
3 tablespoons low-salt salsa,	tortillas

In a medium bowl, thoroughly mix the egg whites, egg, avocado, red pepper, salsa, and cheese. Place the tortillas on a work surface and evenly divide the filling among them. Fold in the edges and roll up. Secure the burritos with toothpicks if necessary. Put the burritos in the air fryer basket. Air fry at 200°C for 3 to 5 minutes, or until the burritos are light golden brown and crisp. Serve with more salsa (if using).

Puffed Egg Tarts

Prep time: 10 minutes | Cook time: 42 minutes | Makes 4 tarts

Oil, for spraying	4 large eggs
Plain flour, for dusting	2 teaspoons chopped fresh
1 (340 g) sheet frozen puff	parsley
pastry, thawed	Salt and freshly ground black
180 ml shredded Cheddar	pepper, to taste
cheese, divided	

Preheat the air fryer to 200°C. Line the air fryer basket with parchment and spray lightly with oil. Lightly dust your work surface with flour. Unfold the puff pastry and cut it into 4 equal squares. Place 2 squares in the prepared basket. Cook for 10 minutes. Remove the basket. Press the centre of each tart shell with a spoon to make an indentation. Sprinkle 3 tablespoons of cheese into each indentation and crack 1 egg into the centre of each tart shell. Cook for another 7 to 11 minutes, or until the eggs are cooked to your desired doneness. Repeat with the remaining puff pastry squares, cheese, and eggs. Sprinkle evenly with the parsley, and season with salt and black pepper. Serve immediately.

Pork Burgers with Red Cabbage Salad

Prep time: 20 minutes | Cook time: 7 to 9 minutes | Serves 4

120 ml Greek yoghurt

2 tablespoons low-salt mustard, divided

1 tablespoon lemon juice

60 ml sliced red cabbage

60 ml grated carrots

450 g lean minced pork

½ teaspoon paprika

235 ml mixed baby lettuce greens

2 small tomatoes, sliced

8 small low-salt wholemeal sandwich buns, cut in half

In a small bowl, combine the yoghurt, 1 tablespoon mustard, lemon juice, cabbage, and carrots; mix and refrigerate. In a medium bowl, combine the pork, remaining 1 tablespoon mustard, and paprika. Form into 8 small patties. Put the sliders into the air fryer basket. Air fry at 204°C for 7 to 9 minutes, or until the sliders register 74°C as tested with a meat thermometer. Assemble the burgers by placing some of the lettuce greens on a bun bottom. Top with a tomato slice, the burgers, and the cabbage mixture. Add the bun top and serve immediately.

Meatball Subs

Prep time: 15 minutes | Cook time: 19 minutes | Serves 6

Oil, for spraying

450 g 15% fat minced beef

120 ml Italian breadcrumbs (mixed breadcrumbs, Italian seasoning and salt)

1 tablespoon dried minced onion

1 tablespoon minced garlic

1 large egg

1 teaspoon salt

1 teaspoon freshly ground black pepper

6 sub rolls

1 (510 g) jar marinara sauce

350 ml shredded Mozzarella cheese

Oil, for spraying 450 g 15% fat minced beef 120 ml Italian breadcrumbs (mixed breadcrumbs, Italian seasoning and salt) 1 tablespoon dried minced onion 1 tablespoon minced garlic 1 large egg 1 teaspoon salt 1 teaspoon freshly ground black pepper 6 sub rolls 1 (510 g) jar marinara sauce 350 ml shredded Mozzarella cheese

Chapter 6 Vegetables and Sides

Tofu Bites

Prep time: 15 minutes | Cook time: 30 minutes | Serves 4

1 packaged firm tofu, cubed and pressed to remove excess water
1 tablespoon soy sauce
1 tablespoon ketchup
1 tablespoon maple syrup
½ teaspoon vinegar
1 teaspoon liquid smoke

1 teaspoon hot sauce
2 tablespoons sesame seeds
1 teaspoon garlic powder
Salt and ground black pepper, to taste
Cooking spray

Preheat the air fryer to 192°C. Spritz a baking dish with cooking spray. Combine all the ingredients to coat the tofu completely and allow the marinade to absorb for half an hour. Transfer the tofu to the baking dish, then air fry for 15 minutes. Flip the tofu over and air fry for another 15 minutes on the other side. Serve immediately.

Cheese-Walnut Stuffed Mushrooms

Prep time: 5 minutes | Cook time: 10 minutes | Serves 4

4 large portobello mushrooms
1 tablespoon rapeseed oil
110 g shredded Mozzarella cheese

35 g minced walnuts
2 tablespoons chopped fresh parsley
Cooking spray

Preheat the air fryer to 180°C. Spritz the air fryer basket with cooking spray. On a clean work surface, remove the mushroom stems. Scoop out the gills with a spoon and discard. Coat the mushrooms with rapeseed oil. Top each mushroom evenly with the shredded Mozzarella cheese, followed by the minced walnuts. Arrange the mushrooms in the air fryer and roast for 10 minutes until golden brown. Transfer the mushrooms to a plate and sprinkle the parsley on top for garnish before serving.

Bacon Potatoes and Green Beans

Prep time: 10 minutes | Cook time: 25 minutes | Serves 4

Oil, for spraying
900 g medium Maris Piper potatoes, quartered
100 g bacon bits

280 g fresh green beans
1 teaspoon salt
½ teaspoon freshly ground black pepper

Line the air fryer basket with parchment and spray lightly with oil.

Place the potatoes in the prepared basket. Top with the bacon bits and green beans. Sprinkle with the salt and black pepper and spray liberally with oil. Air fry at 180°C for 25 minutes, stirring after 12 minutes and spraying with oil, until the potatoes are easily pierced with a fork.

Roasted Brussels Sprouts with Orange and Garlic

Prep time: 5 minutes | Cook time: 10 minutes | Serves 4

450 g Brussels sprouts, quartered
2 garlic cloves, minced

2 tablespoons olive oil
½ teaspoon salt
1 orange, cut into rings

Preheat the air fryer to 180°C. In a large bowl, toss the quartered Brussels sprouts with the garlic, olive oil, and salt until well coated. Pour the Brussels sprouts into the air fryer, lay the orange slices on top of them, and roast for 10 minutes. Remove from the air fryer and set the orange slices aside. Toss the Brussels sprouts before serving.

Easy Greek Briami (Ratatouille)

Prep time: 15 minutes | Cook time: 40 minutes | Serves 6

2 Maris Piper potatoes, cubed
100 g plum tomatoes, cubed
1 aubergine, cubed
1 courgette, cubed
1 red onion, chopped
1 red pepper, chopped
2 garlic cloves, minced
1 teaspoon dried mint
1 teaspoon dried parsley

1 teaspoon dried oregano
½ teaspoon salt
½ teaspoon black pepper
¼ teaspoon red pepper flakes
80 ml olive oil
1 (230 g) can tomato paste
65 ml vegetable stock
65 ml water

Preheat the air fryer to 160°C. In a large bowl, combine the potatoes, tomatoes, aubergine, courgette onion, bell pepper, garlic, mint, parsley, oregano, salt, black pepper, and red pepper flakes. In a small bowl, mix together the olive oil, tomato paste, stock, and water. Pour the oil-and-tomato-paste mixture over the vegetables and toss until everything is coated. Pour the coated vegetables into the air fryer basket in an even layer and roast for 20 minutes. After 20 minutes, stir well and spread out again. Roast for an additional 10 minutes, then repeat the process and cook for another 10 minutes.

Courgette Fritters

Prep time: 10 minutes | Cook time: 10 minutes | Serves 4

2 courgette, grated (about 450 g)	¼ teaspoon dried thyme
1 teaspoon salt	¼ teaspoon ground turmeric
25 g almond flour	¼ teaspoon freshly ground black pepper
20 g grated Parmesan cheese	1 tablespoon olive oil
1 large egg	½ lemon, sliced into wedges

Preheat the air fryer to 200ºC. Cut a piece of parchment paper to fit slightly smaller than the bottom of the air fryer. Place the courgette in a large colander and sprinkle with the salt. Let sit for 5 to 10 minutes. Squeeze as much liquid as you can from the courgette and place in a large mixing bowl. Add the almond flour, Parmesan, egg, thyme, turmeric, and black pepper. Stir gently until thoroughly combined. Shape the mixture into 8 patties and arrange on the parchment paper. Brush lightly with the olive oil. Pausing halfway through the cooking time to turn the patties, air fry for 10 minutes until golden brown. Serve warm with the lemon wedges.

Fried Asparagus

Prep time: 5 minutes | Cook time: 12 minutes | Serves 4

1 tablespoon olive oil	¼ teaspoon ground black pepper
450 g asparagus spears, ends trimmed	1 tablespoon salted butter, melted
¼ teaspoon salt	

In a large bowl, drizzle olive oil over asparagus spears and sprinkle with salt and pepper. Place spears into ungreased air fryer basket. Adjust the temperature to 192ºC and set the timer for 12 minutes, shaking the basket halfway through cooking. Asparagus will be lightly browned and tender when done. Transfer to a large dish and drizzle with butter. Serve warm.

Lemony Broccoli

Prep time: 10 minutes | Cook time: 9 to 14 minutes per batch | Serves 4

1 large head broccoli, rinsed and patted dry	1 tablespoon freshly squeezed lemon juice
2 teaspoons extra-virgin olive oil	Olive oil spray

Cut off the broccoli florets and separate them. You can use the stems, too; peel the stems and cut them into 1-inch chunks. Insert the crisper plate into the basket and the basket into the unit. Preheat the unit by selecting AIR ROAST, setting the temperature to 200ºC, and setting the time to 3 minutes. Select START/STOP to begin.

In a large bowl, toss together the broccoli, olive oil, and lemon juice until coated. Once the unit is preheated, spray the crisper plate with olive oil. Working in batches, place half the broccoli into the basket. Select AIR ROAST, set the temperature to 200ºC, and set the time to 14 minutes. Select START/STOP to begin. After 5 minutes, remove the basket and shake the broccoli. Reinsert the basket to resume cooking. Check the broccoli after 5 minutes. If it is crisp-tender and slightly brown around the edges, it is done. If not, resume cooking. When the cooking is complete, transfer the broccoli to a serving bowl. Repeat steps 5 and 6 with the remaining broccoli. Serve immediately.

Mushrooms with Goat Cheese

Prep time: 10 minutes | Cook time: 10 minutes | Serves 4

3 tablespoons vegetable oil	½ teaspoon black pepper
450 g mixed mushrooms, trimmed and sliced	110 g goat cheese, diced
1 clove garlic, minced	2 teaspoons chopped fresh thyme leaves (optional)
¼ teaspoon dried thyme	

In a baking pan, combine the oil, mushrooms, garlic, dried thyme, and pepper. Stir in the goat cheese. Place the pan in the air fryer basket. Set the air fryer to 200ºC for 10 minutes, stirring halfway through the cooking time. Sprinkle with fresh thyme, if desired.

Blackened Courgette with Kimchi-Herb Sauce

Prep time: 10 minutes | Cook time: 15 minutes | Serves 2

2 medium courgettes, ends trimmed (about 170 g each)	garnish
2 tablespoons olive oil	2 tablespoons rice vinegar
75 g kimchi, finely chopped	2 teaspoons Asian chili-garlic sauce
5 g finely chopped fresh coriander	1 teaspoon grated fresh ginger
5 g finely chopped fresh flat-leaf parsley, plus more for	coarse sea salt and freshly ground black pepper, to taste

Brush the courgettes with half of the olive oil, place in the air fryer, and air fry at 200ºC, turning halfway through, until lightly charred on the outside and tender, about 15 minutes. Meanwhile, in a small bowl, combine the remaining 1 tablespoon olive oil, the kimchi, coriander, parsley, vinegar, chili-garlic sauce, and ginger. Once the courgette is finished cooking, transfer it to a colander and let it cool for 5 minutes. Using your fingers, pinch and break the courgette into bite-size pieces, letting them fall back into the colander. Season the courgette with salt and pepper, toss to combine, then let sit a further 5 minutes to allow some of its liquid to drain. Pile the courgette atop the kimchi sauce on a plate and sprinkle with more parsley to serve.

Mediterranean Courgette Boats

Prep time: 5 minutes | Cook time: 10 minutes |
Serves 4

1 large courgette, ends removed, halved lengthwise	65 g feta cheese
6 grape tomatoes, quartered	1 tablespoon balsamic vinegar
¼ teaspoon salt	1 tablespoon olive oil

Use a spoon to scoop out 2 tablespoons from centre of each courgette half, making just enough space to fill with tomatoes and feta. Place tomatoes evenly in centres of courgette halves and sprinkle with salt. Place into ungreased air fryer basket. Adjust the temperature to 180°C and roast for 10 minutes. When done, courgette will be tender. Transfer boats to a serving tray and sprinkle with feta, then drizzle with vinegar and olive oil. Serve warm.

Rosemary New Potatoes

Prep time: 10 minutes | Cook time: 5 to 6 minutes |
Serves 4

3 large red potatoes	⅛ teaspoon ground black pepper
¼ teaspoon ground rosemary	
¼ teaspoon ground thyme	2 teaspoons extra-light olive oil
⅛ teaspoon salt	

Preheat the air fryer to 170°C. Place potatoes in large bowl and sprinkle with rosemary, thyme, salt, and pepper. Stir with a spoon to distribute seasonings evenly. Add oil to potatoes and stir again to coat well. Air fry at 170°C for 4 minutes. Stir and break apart any that have stuck together. Cook an additional 1 to 2 minutes or until fork-tender.

Asian Tofu Salad

Prep time: 25 minutes | Cook time: 15 minutes | Serves 2

Tofu:	1 tablespoon sugar
1 tablespoon soy sauce	1 teaspoon salt
1 tablespoon vegetable oil	1 teaspoon black pepper
1 teaspoon minced fresh ginger	25 g sliced spring onions
1 teaspoon minced garlic	120 g julienned cucumber
230 g extra-firm tofu, drained and cubed	50 g julienned red onion
Salad:	130 g julienned carrots
60 ml rice vinegar	6 butter lettuce leaves

For the tofu: In a small bowl, whisk together the soy sauce, vegetable oil, ginger, and garlic. Add the tofu and mix gently. Let stand at room temperature for 10 minutes. Arrange the tofu in a single layer in the air fryer basket. Set the air fryer to 200°C for 15 minutes, shaking halfway through the cooking time. Meanwhile, for the salad: In a large bowl, whisk together the vinegar, sugar, salt, pepper, and spring onions. Add the cucumber, onion, and carrots and toss to combine. Set aside to marinate while the tofu cooks. To serve, arrange three lettuce leaves on each of two plates. Pile the marinated vegetables (and marinade) on the lettuce. Divide the tofu between the plates and serve.

Dill-and-Garlic Beetroots

Prep time: 10 minutes | Cook time: 30 minutes | Serves 4

4 beetroots, cleaned, peeled, and sliced	dill
	¼ teaspoon salt
1 garlic clove, minced	¼ teaspoon black pepper
2 tablespoons chopped fresh	3 tablespoons olive oil

Preheat the air fryer to 192°C. In a large bowl, mix together all of the ingredients so the beetroots are well coated with the oil. Pour the beetroot mixture into the air fryer basket, and roast for 15 minutes before stirring, then continue roasting for 15 minutes more.

Garlic Herb Radishes

Prep time: 10 minutes | Cook time: 10 minutes | Serves 4

450 g radishes	½ teaspoon dried parsley
2 tablespoons unsalted butter, melted	¼ teaspoon dried oregano
	¼ teaspoon ground black pepper
½ teaspoon garlic powder	

Remove roots from radishes and cut into quarters. In a small bowl, add butter and seasonings. Toss the radishes in the herb butter and place into the air fryer basket. Adjust the temperature to 180°C and set the timer for 10 minutes. Halfway through the cooking time, toss the radishes in the air fryer basket. Continue cooking until edges begin to turn brown. Serve warm.

Burger Bun for One

Prep time: 2 minutes | Cook time: 5 minutes | Serves 1

2 tablespoons salted butter, melted	¼ teaspoon baking powder
	⅛ teaspoon apple cider vinegar
25 g blanched finely ground almond flour	1 large egg, whisked

Pour butter into an ungreased ramekin. Add flour, baking powder, and vinegar to ramekin and stir until combined. Add egg and stir until batter is mostly smooth. Place ramekin into air fryer basket. Adjust the temperature to 180°C and bake for 5 minutes. When done, the centre will be firm and the top slightly browned. Let cool, about 5 minutes, then remove from ramekin and slice in half. Serve.

Lemon-Garlic Mushrooms

Prep time: 10 minutes | Cook time: 10 to 15 minutes | Serves 6

340 g sliced mushrooms	1 teaspoon freshly squeezed
1 tablespoon avocado oil	lemon juice
Sea salt and freshly ground	½ teaspoon red pepper flakes
black pepper, to taste	2 tablespoons chopped fresh
3 tablespoons unsalted butter	parsley
1 teaspoon minced garlic	

Place the mushrooms in a medium bowl and toss with the oil. Season to taste with salt and pepper. Place the mushrooms in a single layer in the air fryer basket. Set your air fryer to 192°C and roast for 10 to 15 minutes, until the mushrooms are tender. While the mushrooms cook, melt the butter in a small pot or skillet over medium-low heat. Stir in the garlic and cook for 30 seconds. Remove the pot from the heat and stir in the lemon juice and red pepper flakes. Toss the mushrooms with the lemon-garlic butter and garnish with the parsley before serving.

Asparagus Fries

Prep time: 15 minutes | Cook time: 5 to 7 minutes per batch | Serves 4

340 g fresh asparagus spears	25 g grated Parmesan cheese,
with tough ends trimmed off	plus 2 tablespoons
2 egg whites	¼ teaspoon salt
60 ml water	Oil for misting or cooking spray
80 g panko bread crumbs	

Preheat the air fryer to 200°C. In a shallow dish, beat egg whites and water until slightly foamy. In another shallow dish, combine panko, Parmesan, and salt. Dip asparagus spears in egg, then roll in crumbs. Spray with oil or cooking spray. Place a layer of asparagus in air fryer basket, leaving just a little space in between each spear. Stack another layer on top, crosswise. Air fry at 200°C for 5 to 7 minutes, until crispy and golden brown. Repeat to cook remaining asparagus.

Broccoli-Cheddar Twice-Baked Potatoes

Prep time: 10 minutes | Cook time: 46 minutes | Serves 4

Oil, for spraying	1 tablespoon sour cream
2 medium Maris Piper potatoes	1 teaspoon garlic powder
1 tablespoon olive oil	1 teaspoon onion powder
30 g broccoli florets	60 g shredded Cheddar cheese

Line the air fryer basket with parchment and spray lightly with oil. Rinse the potatoes and pat dry with paper towels. Rub the outside of the potatoes with the olive oil and place them in the prepared basket. Air fry at 200°C for 40 minutes, or until easily pierced with a fork. Let cool just enough to handle, then cut the potatoes in half lengthwise. Meanwhile, place the broccoli in a microwave-safe bowl, cover with water, and microwave on high for 5 to 8 minutes. Drain and set aside. Scoop out most of the potato flesh and transfer to a medium bowl. Add the sour cream, garlic, and onion powder and stir until the potatoes are mashed. Spoon the potato mixture back into the hollowed potato skins, mounding it to fit, if necessary. Top with the broccoli and cheese. Return the potatoes to the basket. You may need to work in batches, depending on the size of your air fryer. Air fry at 200°C for 3 to 6 minutes, or until the cheese has melted. Serve immediately.

Golden Pickles

Prep time: 10 minutes | Cook time: 15 minutes | Serves 4

14 dill pickles, sliced	tablespoons water
30 g flour	6 tablespoons panko bread
⅛ teaspoon baking powder	crumbs
Pinch of salt	½ teaspoon paprika
2 tablespoons cornflour plus 3	Cooking spray

Preheat the air fryer to 200°C. Drain any excess moisture out of the dill pickles on a paper towel. In a bowl, combine the flour, baking powder and salt. Throw in the cornflour and water mixture and combine well with a whisk. Put the panko bread crumbs in a shallow dish along with the paprika. Mix thoroughly. Dip the pickles in the flour batter, before coating in the bread crumbs. Spritz all the pickles with the cooking spray. Transfer to the air fryer basket and air fry for 15 minutes, or until golden brown. Serve immediately.

Sesame Taj Tofu

Prep time: 5 minutes | Cook time: 25 minutes | Serves 4

1 block firm tofu, pressed and	seeds
cut into 1-inch thick cubes	1 teaspoon rice vinegar
2 tablespoons soy sauce	1 tablespoon cornflour
2 teaspoons toasted sesame	

Preheat the air fryer to 200°C. Add the tofu, soy sauce, sesame seeds, and rice vinegar in a bowl together and mix well to coat the tofu cubes. Then cover the tofu in cornflour and put it in the air fryer basket. Air fry for 25 minutes, giving the basket a shake at five-minute intervals to ensure the tofu cooks evenly. Serve immediately.

Turnip Fries

Prep time: 10 minutes | Cook time: 20 to 30 minutes | Serves 4

900 g turnip, peeled and cut into ¼ to ½-inch fries

2 tablespoons olive oil

Salt and freshly ground black pepper, to taste

Preheat the air fryer to 200°C. In a large bowl, combine the turnip and olive oil. Season to taste with salt and black pepper. Toss gently until thoroughly coated. Working in batches if necessary, spread the turnip in a single layer in the air fryer basket. Pausing halfway through the cooking time to shake the basket, air fry for 20 to 30 minutes until the fries are lightly browned and crunchy.

Baked Jalapeño and Cheese Cauliflower Mash

Prep time: 10 minutes | Cook time: 15 minutes | Serves 6

1 (340 g) steamer bag cauliflower florets, cooked according to package instructions

2 tablespoons salted butter, softened

60 g cream cheese, softened

120 g shredded sharp Cheddar cheese

20 g pickled jalapeños

½ teaspoon salt

¼ teaspoon ground black pepper

Place cooked cauliflower into a food processor with remaining ingredients. Pulse twenty times until cauliflower is smooth and all ingredients are combined. Spoon mash into an ungreased round nonstick baking dish. Place dish into air fryer basket. Adjust the temperature to 192°C and bake for 15 minutes. The top will be golden brown when done. Serve warm.

Curry Roasted Cauliflower

Prep time: 10 minutes | Cook time: 20 minutes | Serves 4

65 ml olive oil

2 teaspoons curry powder

½ teaspoon salt

¼ teaspoon freshly ground black pepper

1 head cauliflower, cut into bite-size florets

½ red onion, sliced

2 tablespoons freshly chopped parsley, for garnish (optional)

Preheat the air fryer to 200°C. In a large bowl, combine the olive oil, curry powder, salt, and pepper. Add the cauliflower and onion. Toss gently until the vegetables are completely coated with the oil mixture. Transfer the vegetables to the basket of the air fryer. Pausing about halfway through the cooking time to shake the basket, air fry for 20 minutes until the cauliflower is tender and beginning to brown. Top with the parsley, if desired, before serving.

Hawaiian Brown Rice

Prep time: 10 minutes | Cook time: 12 to 16 minutes | Serves 4 to 6

110 g ground sausage

1 teaspoon butter

20 g minced onion

40 g minced bell pepper

380 g cooked brown rice

1 (230 g) can crushed pineapple, drained

Shape sausage into 3 or 4 thin patties. Air fry at 200°C for 6 to 8 minutes or until well done. Remove from air fryer, drain, and crumble. Set aside. Place butter, onion, and bell pepper in baking pan. Roast at 200°C for 1 minute and stir. Cook 3 to 4 minutes longer or just until vegetables are tender. Add sausage, rice, and pineapple to vegetables and stir together. Roast for 2 to 3 minutes, until heated through.

Crispy Garlic Sliced Aubergine

Prep time: 5 minutes | Cook time: 25 minutes | Serves 4

1 egg

1 tablespoon water

60 g whole wheat bread crumbs

1 teaspoon garlic powder

½ teaspoon dried oregano

½ teaspoon salt

½ teaspoon paprika

1 medium aubergine, sliced into ¼-inch-thick rounds

1 tablespoon olive oil

Preheat the air fryer to 180°C. In a medium shallow bowl, beat together the egg and water until frothy. In a separate medium shallow bowl, mix together bread crumbs, garlic powder, oregano, salt, and paprika. Dip each aubergine slice into the egg mixture, then into the bread crumb mixture, coating the outside with crumbs. Place the slices in a single layer in the bottom of the air fryer basket. Drizzle the tops of the aubergine slices with the olive oil, then fry for 15 minutes. Turn each slice and cook for an additional 10 minutes.

Roasted Potatoes and Asparagus

Prep time: 5 minutes | Cook time: 23 minutes | Serves 4

4 medium potatoes

1 bunch asparagus

75 g cottage cheese

80 g low-fat crème fraiche

1 tablespoon wholegrain mustard

Salt and pepper, to taste

Cooking spray

Preheat the air fryer to 200°C. Spritz the air fryer basket with cooking spray. Place the potatoes in the basket. Air fry the potatoes for 20 minutes. Boil the asparagus in salted water for 3 minutes. Remove the potatoes and mash them with rest of ingredients. Sprinkle with salt and pepper. Serve immediately.

Cauliflower with Lime Juice

Prep time: 10 minutes | Cook time: 7 minutes | Serves 4

215 g chopped cauliflower florets
2 tablespoons coconut oil, melted
2 teaspoons chili powder

½ teaspoon garlic powder
1 medium lime
2 tablespoons chopped coriander

In a large bowl, toss cauliflower with coconut oil. Sprinkle with chili powder and garlic powder. Place seasoned cauliflower into the air fryer basket. Adjust the temperature to 180°C and set the timer for 7 minutes. Cauliflower will be tender and begin to turn golden at the edges. Place into a serving bowl. Cut the lime into quarters and squeeze juice over cauliflower. Garnish with coriander.

Corn Croquettes

Prep time: 10 minutes | Cook time: 12 to 14 minutes | Serves 4

105 g leftover mashed potatoes
340 g corn kernels (if frozen, thawed, and well drained)
¼ teaspoon onion powder
⅛ teaspoon ground black pepper

¼ teaspoon salt
50 g panko bread crumbs
Oil for misting or cooking spray

Place the potatoes and half the corn in food processor and pulse until corn is well chopped. Transfer mixture to large bowl and stir in remaining corn, onion powder, pepper and salt. Shape mixture into 16 balls. Roll balls in panko crumbs, mist with oil or cooking spray, and place in air fryer basket. Air fry at 180°C for 12 to 14 minutes, until golden brown and crispy

Cheesy Loaded Broccoli

Prep time: 10 minutes | Cook time: 10 minutes | Serves 2

215 g fresh broccoli florets
1 tablespoon coconut oil
¼ teaspoon salt
120 g shredded sharp Cheddar cheese

60 g sour cream
4 slices cooked sugar-free bacon, crumbled
1 medium spring onion, trimmed and sliced on the bias

Place broccoli into ungreased air fryer basket, drizzle with coconut oil, and sprinkle with salt. Adjust the temperature to 180°C and roast for 8 minutes. Shake basket three times during cooking to avoid burned spots. Sprinkle broccoli with Cheddar and cook for 2 additional minutes. When done, cheese will be melted and broccoli will be tender. Serve warm in a large serving dish, topped with sour cream, crumbled bacon, and spring onion slices.

Chapter 7 Poultry

Spanish Chicken and Mini Sweet Pepper Baguette

Prep time: 10 minutes | Cook time: 20 minutes | Serves 2

570 g assorted small chicken parts, breasts cut into halves	230 g mini sweet peppers
¼ teaspoon salt	60 g light mayonnaise
¼ teaspoon ground black pepper	¼ teaspoon smoked paprika
	½ clove garlic, crushed
2 teaspoons olive oil	Baguette, for serving
	Cooking spray

Preheat air fryer to 190°C. Spritz the air fryer basket with cooking spray. Toss the chicken with salt, ground black pepper, and olive oil in a large bowl. Arrange the sweet peppers and chicken in the preheated air fryer and air fry for 10 minutes, then transfer the peppers on a plate. Flip the chicken and air fry for 10 more minutes or until well browned. Meanwhile, combine the mayo, paprika, and garlic in a small bowl. Stir to mix well. Assemble the baguette with chicken and sweet pepper, then spread with mayo mixture and serve.

Chicken Burgers with Ham and Cheese

Prep time: 12 minutes | Cook time: 13 to 16 minutes | Serves 4

40 g soft bread crumbs	taste
3 tablespoons milk	570 g chicken mince
1 egg, beaten	70 g finely chopped ham
½ teaspoon dried thyme	75 g grated Gouda cheese
Pinch salt	Olive oil for misting
Freshly ground black pepper, to	

Preheat the air fryer to 180°C. In a medium bowl, combine the bread crumbs, milk, egg, thyme, salt, and pepper. Add the chicken and mix gently but thoroughly with clean hands. Form the chicken into eight thin patties and place on waxed paper. Top four of the patties with the ham and cheese. Top with remaining four patties and gently press the edges together to seal, so the ham and cheese mixture is in the middle of the burger. Place the burgers in the basket and mist with olive oil. Bake for 13 to 16 minutes or until the chicken is thoroughly cooked to 76°C as measured with a meat thermometer. Serve immediately.

Butter and Bacon Chicken

Prep time: 10 minutes | Cook time: 65 minutes | Serves 6

1 (1.8 kg) whole chicken	1 teaspoon salt
2 tablespoons salted butter, softened	½ teaspoon ground black pepper
1 teaspoon dried thyme	6 slices sugar-free bacon
½ teaspoon garlic powder	

Pat chicken dry with a paper towel, then rub with butter on all sides. Sprinkle thyme, garlic powder, salt, and pepper over chicken. Place chicken into ungreased air fryer basket, breast side up. Lay strips of bacon over chicken and secure with toothpicks. Adjust the temperature to 180°C and air fry for 65 minutes. Halfway through cooking, remove and set aside bacon and flip chicken over. Chicken will be done when the skin is golden and crispy and the internal temperature is at least 76°C. Serve warm with bacon.

Chicken Croquettes with Creole Sauce

Prep time: 30 minutes | Cook time: 10 minutes | Serves 4

280 g shredded cooked chicken	Creole Sauce:
120 g shredded Cheddar cheese	60 g mayonnaise
2 eggs	60 g sour cream
15 g finely chopped onion	1½ teaspoons Dijon mustard
25 g almond meal	1½ teaspoons fresh lemon juice
1 tablespoon poultry seasoning	½ teaspoon garlic powder
Olive oil	½ teaspoon Creole seasoning

In a large bowl, combine the chicken, Cheddar, eggs, onion, almond meal, and poultry seasoning. Stir gently until thoroughly combined. Cover and refrigerate for 30 minutes. Meanwhile, to make the Creole sauce: In a small bowl, whisk together the mayonnaise, sour cream, Dijon mustard, lemon juice, garlic powder, and Creole seasoning until thoroughly combined. Cover and refrigerate until ready to serve. Preheat the air fryer to 200°C. Divide the chicken mixture into 8 portions and shape into patties. Working in batches if necessary, arrange the patties in a single layer in the air fryer basket and coat both sides lightly with olive oil. Pausing halfway through the cooking time to flip the patties, air fry for 10 minutes, or until lightly browned and the cheese is melted. Serve with the Creole sauce.

Wild Rice and Kale Stuffed Chicken Thighs

Prep time: 10 minutes | Cook time: 22 minutes | Serves 4

4 boneless, skinless chicken thighs
250 g cooked wild rice
35 g chopped kale
2 garlic cloves, minced

1 teaspoon salt
Juice of 1 lemon
100 g crumbled feta
Olive oil cooking spray
1 tablespoon olive oi

Preheat the air fryer to 192ºC. Place the chicken thighs between two pieces of plastic wrap, and using a meat mallet or a rolling pin, pound them out to about ¼-inch thick. In a medium bowl, combine the rice, kale, garlic, salt, and lemon juice and mix well. Place a quarter of the rice mixture into the middle of each chicken thigh, then sprinkle 2 tablespoons of feta over the filling. Spray the air fryer basket with olive oil cooking spray. Fold the sides of the chicken thigh over the filling, and then gently place each of them seam-side down into the air fryer basket. Brush each stuffed chicken thigh with olive oil. Roast the stuffed chicken thighs for 12 minutes, then turn them over and cook for an additional 10 minutes, or until the internal temperature reaches 76ºC.

Chicken Paillard

Prep time: 10 minutes | Cook time: 10 minutes | Serves 2

2 large eggs, room temperature
1 tablespoon water
40 g powdered Parmesan cheese or pork dust
2 teaspoons dried thyme leaves
1 teaspoon ground black pepper
2 (140 g) boneless, skinless chicken breasts, pounded to ½ inch thick

Lemon Butter Sauce:
2 tablespoons unsalted butter, melted
2 teaspoons lemon juice
¼ teaspoon finely chopped fresh thyme leaves, plus more for garnish
⅛ teaspoon fine sea salt
Lemon slices, for serving

Spray the air fryer basket with avocado oil. Preheat the air fryer to 200ºC. Beat the eggs in a shallow dish, then add the water and stir well. In a separate shallow dish, mix together the Parmesan, thyme, and pepper until well combined. One at a time, dip the chicken breasts in the eggs and let any excess drip off, then dredge both sides of the chicken in the Parmesan mixture. As you finish, set the coated chicken in the air fryer basket. Roast the chicken in the air fryer for 5 minutes, then flip the chicken and cook for another 5 minutes, or until cooked through and the internal temperature reaches 76ºC. While the chicken cooks, make the lemon butter sauce: In a small bowl, mix together all the sauce ingredients until well combined. Plate the chicken and pour the sauce over it. Garnish with chopped fresh thyme and serve with lemon slices. Store leftovers in an airtight container in the refrigerator for up to 4 days. Reheat in a preheated 200ºC air fryer for 5 minutes, or until heated through.

Tex-Mex Chicken Roll-Ups

Prep time: 10 minutes | Cook time: 14 to 17 minutes | Serves 8

900 g boneless, skinless chicken breasts or thighs
1 teaspoon chili powder
½ teaspoon smoked paprika
½ teaspoon ground cumin
Sea salt and freshly ground

black pepper, to taste
170 g Monterey Jack cheese, shredded
115 g canned diced green chilies
Avocado oil spray

Place the chicken in a large zip-top bag or between two pieces of plastic wrap. Using a meat mallet or heavy skillet, pound the chicken until it is about ¼ inch thick. In a small bowl, combine the chili powder, smoked paprika, cumin, and salt and pepper to taste. Sprinkle both sides of the chicken with the seasonings. Sprinkle the chicken with the Monterey Jack cheese, then the diced green chilies. Roll up each piece of chicken from the long side, tucking in the ends as you go. Secure the roll-up with a toothpick. Set the air fryer to 180ºC. . Spray the outside of the chicken with avocado oil. Place the chicken in a single layer in the basket, working in batches if necessary, and roast for 7 minutes. Flip and cook for another 7 to 10 minutes, until an instant-read thermometer reads 70ºC. Remove the chicken from the air fryer and allow it to rest for about 5 minutes before serving.

Barbecued Chicken with Creamy Coleslaw

Prep time: 10 minutes | Cook time: 20 minutes | Serves 2

270 g shredded coleslaw mix
Salt and pepper
2 (340 g) bone-in split chicken breasts, trimmed
1 teaspoon vegetable oil
2 tablespoons barbecue sauce,

plus extra for serving
2 tablespoons mayonnaise
2 tablespoons sour cream
1 teaspoon distilled white vinegar, plus extra for seasoning
¼ teaspoon sugar

Preheat the air fryer to 180ºC. Toss coleslaw mix and ¼ teaspoon salt in a colander set over bowl. Let sit until wilted slightly, about 30 minutes. Rinse, drain, and dry well with a dish towel. Meanwhile, pat chicken dry with paper towels, rub with oil, and season with salt and pepper. Arrange breasts skin-side down in air fryer basket, spaced evenly apart, alternating ends. Bake for 10 minutes. Flip breasts and brush skin side with barbecue sauce. Return basket to air fryer and bake until well browned and chicken registers 70ºC, 10 to 15 minutes. Transfer chicken to serving platter, tent loosely with aluminum foil, and let rest for 5 minutes. While chicken rests, whisk mayonnaise, sour cream, vinegar, sugar, and pinch pepper together in a large bowl. Stir in coleslaw mix and season with salt, pepper, and additional vinegar to taste. Serve chicken with coleslaw, passing extra barbecue sauce separately.

Chicken and Broccoli Casserole

Prep time: 5 minutes | Cook time: 20 to 25 minutes | Serves 4

230 g broccoli, chopped into florets	½ teaspoon garlic powder
280 g shredded cooked chicken	Salt and freshly ground black pepper, to taste
115 g cream cheese	2 tablespoons chopped fresh basil
80 g heavy cream	
1½ teaspoons Dijon mustard	230 g shredded Cheddar cheese

Preheat the air fryer to 200°C. Lightly coat a casserole dish that will fit in air fryer, with olive oil and set aside. Place the broccoli in a large glass bowl with 1 tablespoon of water and cover with a microwavable plate. Microwave on high for 2 to 3 minutes until the broccoli is bright green but not mushy. Drain if necessary and add to another large bowl along with the shredded chicken. In the same glass bowl used to microwave the broccoli, combine the cream cheese and cream. Microwave for 30 seconds to 1 minute on high and stir until smooth. Add the mustard and garlic powder and season to taste with salt and freshly ground black pepper. Whisk until the sauce is smooth. Pour the warm sauce over the broccoli and chicken mixture and then add the basil. Using a silicone spatula, gently fold the mixture until thoroughly combined. Transfer the chicken mixture to the prepared casserole dish and top with the cheese. Air fry for 20 to 25 minutes until warmed through and the cheese has browned.

Chicken Breasts with Asparagus, Beans, and Rocket

Prep time: 20 minutes | Cook time: 25 minutes | Serves 2

160 g canned cannellini beans, rinsed	½ red onion, sliced thinly
1½ tablespoons red wine vinegar	230 g asparagus, trimmed and cut into 1-inch lengths
1 garlic clove, minced	2 (230 g) boneless, skinless chicken breasts, trimmed
2 tablespoons extra-virgin olive oil, divided	¼ teaspoon paprika
Salt and ground black pepper, to taste	½ teaspoon ground coriander
	60 g baby rocket, rinsed and drained

Preheat the air fryer to 200°C. Warm the beans in microwave for 1 minutes and combine with red wine vinegar, garlic, 1 tablespoon of olive oil, ¼ teaspoon of salt, and ¼ teaspoon of ground black pepper in a bowl. Stir to mix well. Combine the onion with ⅛ teaspoon of salt, ⅛ teaspoon of ground black pepper, and 2 teaspoons of olive oil in a separate bowl. Toss to coat well. Place the onion in the air fryer and air fry for 2 minutes, then add the asparagus and air fry for 8 more minutes or until the asparagus is tender. Shake the basket halfway through. Transfer the onion and asparagus to the bowl with beans. Set aside. Toss the chicken breasts with remaining ingredients, except for the baby rocket, in a large bowl. Put the chicken breasts in the air fryer and air fry for 14 minutes or until the internal temperature of the chicken reaches at least 76°C. Flip the breasts halfway through. Remove the chicken from the air fryer and serve on an aluminum foil with asparagus, beans, onion, and rocket. Sprinkle with salt and ground black pepper. Toss to serve.

Fajita-Stuffed Chicken Breast

Prep time: 15 minutes | Cook time: 25 minutes | Serves 4

2 (170 g) boneless, skinless chicken breasts	seeded and sliced
¼ medium white onion, peeled and sliced	1 tablespoon coconut oil
	2 teaspoons chili powder
1 medium green bell pepper,	1 teaspoon ground cumin
	½ teaspoon garlic powder

Slice each chicken breast completely in half lengthwise into two even pieces. Using a meat tenderizer, pound out the chicken until it's about ¼-inch thickness. Lay each slice of chicken out and place three slices of onion and four slices of green pepper on the end closest to you. Begin rolling the peppers and onions tightly into the chicken. Secure the roll with either toothpicks or a couple pieces of butcher's twine. Drizzle coconut oil over chicken. Sprinkle each side with chili powder, cumin, and garlic powder. Place each roll into the air fryer basket. Adjust the temperature to 180°C and air fry for 25 minutes. Serve warm.

Stuffed Turkey Roulade

Prep time: 10 minutes | Cook time: 45 minutes | Serves 4

1 (900 g) boneless turkey breast, skin removed	1 tablespoon fresh sage
1 teaspoon salt	2 garlic cloves, minced
½ teaspoon black pepper	2 tablespoons olive oil
115 g goat cheese	Fresh chopped parsley, for garnish
1 tablespoon fresh thyme	

Preheat the air fryer to 192°C. Using a sharp knife, butterfly the turkey breast, and season both sides with salt and pepper and set aside. In a small bowl, mix together the goat cheese, thyme, sage, and garlic. Spread the cheese mixture over the turkey breast, then roll it up tightly, tucking the ends underneath. Place the turkey breast roulade onto a piece of aluminum foil, wrap it up, and place it into the air fryer. Bake for 30 minutes. Remove the foil from the turkey breast and brush the top with oil, then continue cooking for another 10 to 15 minutes, or until the outside has browned and the internal temperature reaches 76°C. Remove and cut into 1-inch-wide slices and serve with a sprinkle of parsley on top.

Greek Chicken Stir-Fry

Prep time: 15 minutes | Cook time: 15 minutes | Serves 2

1 (170 g) chicken breast, cut into 1-inch cubes	and sliced
	1 tablespoon coconut oil
½ medium courgette, chopped	1 teaspoon dried oregano
½ medium red bell pepper, seeded and chopped	½ teaspoon garlic powder
	¼ teaspoon dried thyme
¼ medium red onion, peeled	

Place all ingredients into a large mixing bowl and toss until the coconut oil coats the meat and vegetables. Pour the contents of the bowl into the air fryer basket. Adjust the temperature to (190°C and air fry for 15 minutes. Shake the basket halfway through the cooking time to redistribute the food. Serve immediately.

Crispy Duck with Cherry Sauce

Prep time: 10 minutes | Cook time: 33 minutes |
Serves 2 to 4

1 whole duck (2.3 kg), split in half, back and rib bones removed	1 shallot, minced
	120 ml sherry
	240 g cherry preserves
1 teaspoon olive oil	240 ml chicken stock
Salt and freshly ground black pepper, to taste	1 teaspoon white wine vinegar
	1 teaspoon fresh thyme leaves
Cherry Sauce:	Salt and freshly ground black pepper, to taste
1 tablespoon butter	

Preheat the air fryer to 200°C. Trim some of the fat from the duck. Rub olive oil on the duck and season with salt and pepper. Place the duck halves in the air fryer basket, breast side up and facing the centre of the basket. Air fry the duck for 20 minutes. Turn the duck over and air fry for another 6 minutes. While duck is air frying, make the cherry sauce. Melt the butter in a large sauté pan. Add the shallot and sauté until it is just starting to brown, about 2 to 3 minutes. Add the sherry and deglaze the pan by scraping up any brown bits from the bottom of the pan. Simmer the liquid for a few minutes, until it has reduced by half. Add the cherry preserves, chicken stock and white wine vinegar. Whisk well to combine all the ingredients. Simmer the sauce until it thickens and coats the back of a spoon, about 5 to 7 minutes. Season with salt and pepper and stir in the fresh thyme leaves. When the air fryer timer goes off, spoon some cherry sauce over the duck and continue to air fry at 200°C for 4 more minutes. Then, turn the duck halves back over so that the breast side is facing up. Spoon more cherry sauce over the top of the duck, covering the skin completely. Air fry for 3 more minutes and then remove the duck to a plate to rest for a few minutes. Serve the duck in halves, or cut each piece in half again for a smaller serving. Spoon any additional sauce over the duck or serve it on the side.

Chicken, Courgette, and Spinach Salad

Prep time: 10 minutes | Cook time: 20 minutes | Serves 4

3 (140 g) boneless, skinless chicken breasts, cut into 1-inch cubes	1 medium red onion, sliced
	1 red bell pepper, sliced
	1 small courgette, cut into strips
5 teaspoons extra-virgin olive oil	3 tablespoons freshly squeezed lemon juice
½ teaspoon dried thyme	85 g fresh baby spinach leaves

Insert the crisper plate into the basket and the basket into the unit. Preheat the unit by selecting AIR ROAST, setting the temperature to 190°C, and setting the time to 3 minutes. Select START/STOP to begin. In a large bowl, combine the chicken, olive oil, and thyme. Toss to coat. Transfer to a medium metal bowl that fits into the basket. Once the unit is preheated, place the bowl into the basket. Select AIR ROAST, set the temperature to 190°C, and set the time to 20 minutes. Select START/STOP to begin. After 8 minutes, add the red onion, red bell pepper, and courgette to the bowl. Resume cooking. After about 6 minutes more, stir the chicken and vegetables. Resume cooking. When the cooking is complete, a food thermometer inserted into the chicken should register at least 76°C. Remove the bowl from the unit and stir in the lemon juice. Put the spinach in a serving bowl and top with the chicken mixture. Toss to combine and serve immediately.

Pecan Turkey Cutlets

Prep time: 10 minutes | Cook time: 10 to 12 minutes
per batch | Serves 4

90 g panko bread crumbs	30 g cornflour
¼ teaspoon salt	1 egg, beaten
¼ teaspoon pepper	450 g turkey cutlets, ½-inch thick
¼ teaspoon mustard powder	
¼ teaspoon poultry seasoning	Salt and pepper, to taste
50 g pecans	Oil for misting or cooking spray

Place the panko crumbs, ¼ teaspoon salt, ¼ teaspoon pepper, mustard, and poultry seasoning in food processor. Process until crumbs are finely crushed. Add pecans and process in short pulses just until nuts are finely chopped. Go easy so you don't overdo it! Preheat the air fryer to 180°C. Place cornflour in one shallow dish and beaten egg in another. Transfer coating mixture from food processor into a third shallow dish. Sprinkle turkey cutlets with salt and pepper to taste. Dip cutlets in cornflour and shake off excess. Then dip in beaten egg and roll in crumbs, pressing to coat well. Spray both sides with oil or cooking spray. Place 2 cutlets in air fryer basket in a single layer and cook for 10 to 12 minutes or until juices run clear. Repeat step 6 to cook remaining cutlets.

Easy Turkey Tenderloin

Prep time: 20 minutes | Cook time: 30 minutes | Serves 4

Olive oil	½ teaspoon freshly ground
½ teaspoon paprika	black pepper
½ teaspoon garlic powder	Pinch cayenne pepper
½ teaspoon salt	680 g turkey breast tenderloin

Spray the air fryer basket lightly with olive oil. In a small bowl, combine the paprika, garlic powder, salt, black pepper, and cayenne pepper. Rub the mixture all over the turkey. Place the turkey in the air fryer basket and lightly spray with olive oil. Air fry at 190°C for 15 minutes. Flip the turkey over and lightly spray with olive oil. Air fry until the internal temperature reaches at least 80°C for an additional 10 to 15 minutes. Let the turkey rest for 10 minutes before slicing and serving.

Buffalo Chicken Cheese Sticks

Prep time: 5 minutes | Cook time: 8 minutes | Serves 2

140 g shredded cooked chicken	cheese
60 ml buffalo sauce	1 large egg
220 g shredded Mozzarella	55 g crumbled feta

In a large bowl, mix all ingredients except the feta. Cut a piece of parchment to fit your air fryer basket and press the mixture into a ½-inch-thick circle. Sprinkle the mixture with feta and place into the air fryer basket. Adjust the temperature to 200°C and air fry for 8 minutes. After 5 minutes, flip over the cheese mixture. Allow to cool 5 minutes before cutting into sticks. Serve warm.

Italian Flavour Chicken Breasts with Roma Tomatoes

Prep time: 10 minutes | Cook time: 60 minutes | Serves 8

1.4 kg chicken breasts, bone-in	½ teaspoon salt
1 teaspoon minced fresh basil	½ teaspoon freshly ground
1 teaspoon minced fresh	black pepper
rosemary	4 medium Roma tomatoes,
2 tablespoons minced fresh	halved
parsley	Cooking spray
1 teaspoon cayenne pepper	

Preheat the air fryer to 190°C. Spritz the air fryer basket with cooking spray. Combine all the ingredients, except for the chicken breasts and tomatoes, in a large bowl. Stir to mix well. Dunk the chicken breasts in the mixture and press to coat well. Transfer the chicken breasts in the preheated air fryer. You may need to work in batches to avoid overcrowding. Air fry for 25 minutes or until the internal temperature of the thickest part of the breasts reaches at least 76°C. Flip the breasts halfway through the cooking time. Remove the cooked chicken breasts from the basket and adjust the temperature to 180°C. Place the tomatoes in the air fryer and spritz with cooking spray. Sprinkle with a touch of salt and cook for 10 minutes or until tender. Shake the basket halfway through the cooking time. Serve the tomatoes with chicken breasts on a large serving plate.

Lemon-Dijon Boneless Chicken

Prep time: 30 minutes | Cook time: 13 to 16 minutes | Serves 6

115 g sugar-free mayonnaise	1 teaspoon sea salt
1 tablespoon Dijon mustard	½ teaspoon freshly ground
1 tablespoon freshly squeezed	black pepper
lemon juice (optional)	¼ teaspoon cayenne pepper
1 tablespoon coconut aminos	680 g boneless, skinless chicken
1 teaspoon Italian seasoning	breasts or thighs

In a small bowl, combine the mayonnaise, mustard, lemon juice (if using), coconut aminos, Italian seasoning, salt, black pepper, and cayenne pepper. Place the chicken in a shallow dish or large zip-top plastic bag. Add the marinade, making sure all the pieces are coated. Cover and refrigerate for at least 30 minutes or up to 4 hours. Set the air fryer to 200°C. Arrange the chicken in a single layer in the air fryer basket, working in batches if necessary. Air fry for 7 minutes. Flip the chicken and continue cooking for 6 to 9 minutes more, until an instant-read thermometer reads 70°C.

Buttermilk-Fried Drumsticks

Prep time: 10 minutes | Cook time: 25 minutes | Serves 2

1 egg	1 teaspoon salt
120 g buttermilk	¼ teaspoon ground black
90 g self-rising flour	pepper (to mix into coating)
90 g seasoned panko bread	4 chicken drumsticks, skin on
crumbs	Oil for misting or cooking spray

Beat together egg and buttermilk in shallow dish. In a second shallow dish, combine the flour, panko crumbs, salt, and pepper. Sprinkle chicken legs with additional salt and pepper to taste. Dip legs in buttermilk mixture, then roll in panko mixture, pressing in crumbs to make coating stick. Mist with oil or cooking spray. Spray the air fryer basket with cooking spray. Cook drumsticks at 180°C for 10 minutes. Turn pieces over and cook an additional 10 minutes. Turn pieces to check for browning. If you have any white spots that haven't begun to brown, spritz them with oil or cooking spray. Continue cooking for 5 more minutes or until crust is golden brown and juices run clear. Larger, meatier drumsticks will take longer to cook than small ones.

Teriyaki Chicken Legs

Prep time: 12 minutes | Cook time: 18 to 20 minutes | Serves 2

4 tablespoons teriyaki sauce	4 chicken legs
1 tablespoon orange juice	Cooking spray
1 teaspoon smoked paprika	

Mix together the teriyaki sauce, orange juice, and smoked paprika. Brush on all sides of chicken legs. Spray the air fryer basket with nonstick cooking spray and place chicken in basket. Air fry at 180°C for 6 minutes. Turn and baste with sauce. Cook for 6 more minutes, turn and baste. Cook for 6 to 8 minutes more, until juices run clear when chicken is pierced with a fork.

Apricot-Glazed Turkey Tenderloin

Prep time: 20 minutes | Cook time: 30 minutes | Serves 4

Olive oil	mustard
80 g sugar-free apricot preserves	680 g turkey breast tenderloin
½ tablespoon spicy brown	Salt and freshly ground black pepper, to taste

Spray the air fryer basket lightly with olive oil. In a small bowl, combine the apricot preserves and mustard to make a paste. Season the turkey with salt and pepper. Spread the apricot paste all over the turkey. Place the turkey in the air fryer basket and lightly spray with olive oil. Air fry at 190°C for 15 minutes. Flip the turkey over and lightly spray with olive oil. Air fry until the internal temperature reaches at least 80°C, an additional 10 to 15 minutes. Let the turkey rest for 10 minutes before slicing and serving.

Tortilla Crusted Chicken Breast

Prep time: 10 minutes | Cook time: 12 minutes | Serves 2

40 g flour	2 (85 to 115 g) boneless chicken breasts
1 teaspoon salt	
1½ teaspoons chili powder	Vegetable oil
1 teaspoon ground cumin	125 g salsa
Freshly ground black pepper, to taste	40 g crumbled feta cheese
1 egg, beaten	Fresh coriander leaves
25 g coarsely crushed yellow corn tortilla chips	Sour cream or guacamole (optional)

Set up a dredging station with three shallow dishes. Combine the flour, salt, chili powder, cumin and black pepper in the first shallow dish. Beat the egg in the second shallow dish. Place the crushed tortilla chips in the third shallow dish. Dredge the chicken in the spiced flour, covering all sides of the breast. Then dip the chicken into the egg, coating the chicken completely. Finally, place the chicken into the tortilla chips and press the chips onto the chicken to make sure they adhere to all sides of the breast. Spray the coated chicken breasts on both sides with vegetable oil. Preheat the air fryer to 190°C. Air fry the chicken for 6 minutes. Then turn the chicken breasts over and air fry for another 6 minutes. (Increase the cooking time if you are using chicken breasts larger than 85 to 115 g.) When the chicken has finished cooking, serve each breast with a little salsa, the crumbled feta and coriander as the finishing touch. Serve some sour cream and/or guacamole at the table, if desired.

Simply Terrific Turkey Meatballs

Prep time: 10 minutes | Cook time: 7 to 10 minutes | Serves 4

1 red bell pepper, seeded and coarsely chopped	1 egg, lightly beaten
2 cloves garlic, coarsely chopped	45 g grated Parmesan cheese
	1 teaspoon salt
15 g chopped fresh parsley	½ teaspoon freshly ground black pepper
680 g 85% lean turkey mince	

Preheat the air fryer to 200°C. In a food processor fitted with a metal blade, combine the bell pepper, garlic, and parsley. Pulse until finely chopped. Transfer the vegetables to a large mixing bowl. Add the turkey, egg, Parmesan, salt, and black pepper. Mix gently until thoroughly combined. Shape the mixture into 1¼-inch meatballs. Working in batches if necessary, arrange the meatballs in a single layer in the air fryer basket; coat lightly with olive oil spray. Pausing halfway through the cooking time to shake the basket, air fry for 7 to 10 minutes, until lightly browned and a thermometer inserted into the centre of a meatball registers 76°C.

Nice Goulash

Prep time: 5 minutes | Cook time: 17 minutes | Serves 2

2 red bell peppers, chopped	Salt and ground black pepper, to taste
450 g chicken mince	
2 medium tomatoes, diced	Cooking spray
120 ml chicken broth	

Preheat the air fryer to 186°C. Spritz a baking pan with cooking spray. Set the bell pepper in the baking pan and put in the air fry to broil for 5 minutes or until the bell pepper is tender. Shake the basket halfway through. Add the chicken mince and diced tomatoes in the baking pan and stir to mix well. Broil for 6 more minutes or until the chicken is lightly browned. Pour the chicken broth over and sprinkle with salt and ground black pepper. Stir to mix well. Broil for an additional 6 minutes. Serve immediately.

Turkey and Cranberry Quesadillas

Prep time: 7 minutes | Cook time: 4 to 8 minutes | Serves 4

6 low-sodium whole-wheat tortillas

75 g shredded low-sodium low-fat Swiss cheese

105 g shredded cooked low-sodium turkey breast

2 tablespoons cranberry sauce

2 tablespoons dried cranberries

½ teaspoon dried basil

Olive oil spray, for spraying the tortillas

Preheat the air fryer to 200ºC. Put 3 tortillas on a work surface. Evenly divide the Swiss cheese, turkey, cranberry sauce, and dried cranberries among the tortillas. Sprinkle with the basil and top with the remaining tortillas. Spray the outsides of the tortillas with olive oil spray. One at a time, air fry the quesadillas in the air fryer for 4 to 8 minutes, or until crisp and the cheese is melted. Cut into quarters and serve.

Thai Chicken with Cucumber and Chili Salad

Prep time: 25 minutes | Cook time: 25 minutes | Serves 6

2 (570 g) small chickens, giblets discarded

1 tablespoon fish sauce

6 tablespoons chopped fresh coriander

2 teaspoons lime zest

1 teaspoon ground coriander

2 garlic cloves, minced

2 tablespoons packed light brown sugar

2 teaspoons vegetable oil

Salt and ground black pepper,

to taste

1 English cucumber, halved lengthwise and sliced thin

1 Thai chili, stemmed, deseeded, and minced

2 tablespoons chopped dry-roasted peanuts

1 small shallot, sliced thinly

1 tablespoon lime juice

Lime wedges, for serving

Cooking spray

Arrange a chicken on a clean work surface, remove the backbone with kitchen shears, then pound the chicken breast to flat. Cut the breast in half. Repeat with the remaining chicken. Loose the breast and thigh skin with your fingers, then pat the chickens dry and pierce about 10 holes into the fat deposits of the chickens. Tuck the wings under the chickens. Combine 2 teaspoons of fish sauce, coriander, lime zest, coriander, garlic, 4 teaspoons of sugar, 1 teaspoon of vegetable oil, ½ teaspoon of salt, and ⅛ teaspoon of ground black pepper in a small bowl. Stir to mix well. Rub the fish sauce mixture under the breast and thigh skin of the game chickens, then let sit for 10 minutes to marinate. Preheat the air fryer to 200ºC. Spritz the air fryer basket with cooking spray. Arrange the marinated chickens in the preheated air fryer, skin side down. Air fry for 15 minutes, then gently turn the game hens over and air fry for 10 more minutes or until the skin is golden brown and the internal temperature of the chickens reads at least 76ºC. Meanwhile,

combine all the remaining ingredients, except for the lime wedges, in a large bowl and sprinkle with salt and black pepper. Toss to mix well. Transfer the fried chickens on a large plate, then sit the salad aside and squeeze the lime wedges over before serving.

Sriracha-Honey Chicken Nuggets

Prep time: 15 minutes | Cook time: 19 minutes | Serves 6

Oil, for spraying

1 large egg

180 ml milk

125 g all-purpose flour

2 tablespoons icing sugar

½ teaspoon paprika

½ teaspoon salt

½ teaspoon freshly ground black pepper

2 boneless, skinless chicken breasts, cut into bite-size pieces

140 g barbecue sauce

2 tablespoons honey

1 tablespoon Sriracha

Line the air fryer basket with parchment and spray lightly with oil. In a small bowl, whisk together the egg and milk. In a medium bowl, combine the flour, icing sugar, paprika, salt, and black pepper and stir. Coat the chicken in the egg mixture, then dredge in the flour mixture until evenly coated. Place the chicken in the prepared basket and spray liberally with oil. Air fry at 200ºC for 8 minutes, flip, spray with more oil, and cook for another 6 to 8 minutes, or until the internal temperature reaches 76ºC and the juices run clear. In a large bowl, mix together the barbecue sauce, honey, and Sriracha. Transfer the chicken to the bowl and toss until well coated with the barbecue sauce mixture. Line the air fryer basket with fresh parchment, return the chicken to the basket, and cook for another 2 to 3 minutes, until browned and crispy.

One-Dish Chicken and Rice

Prep time: 10 minutes | Cook time: 40 minutes | Serves 4

190 g long-grain white rice, rinsed and drained

120 g cut frozen green beans (do not thaw)

1 tablespoon minced fresh ginger

3 cloves garlic, minced

1 tablespoon toasted sesame oil

1 teaspoon kosher salt

1 teaspoon black pepper

450 g chicken wings, preferably drumettes

In a baking pan, combine the rice, green beans, ginger, garlic, sesame oil, salt, and pepper. Stir to combine. Place the chicken wings on top of the rice mixture. Cover the pan with foil. Make a long slash in the foil to allow the pan to vent steam. Place the pan in the air fryer basket. Set the air fryer to (190ºC for 30 minutes. Remove the foil. Set the air fryer to 200ºC for 10 minutes, or until the wings have browned and rendered fat into the rice and vegetables, turning the wings halfway through the cooking time.

Blackened Chicken

Prep time: 10 minutes | Cook time: 20 minutes | Serves 4

1 large egg, beaten
215 g Blackened seasoning
2 whole boneless, skinless

chicken breasts (about 450 g each), halved
1 to 2 tablespoons oil

Place the beaten egg in one shallow bowl and the Blackened seasoning in another shallow bowl. One at a time, dip the chicken pieces in the beaten egg and the Blackened seasoning, coating thoroughly. Preheat the air fryer to 180ºC. Line the air fryer basket with parchment paper. Place the chicken pieces on the parchment and spritz with oil. Cook for 10 minutes. Flip the chicken, spritz it with oil, and cook for 10 minutes more until the internal temperature reaches 76ºC and the chicken is no longer pink inside. Let sit for 5 minutes before serving.

Fajita Chicken Strips

Prep time: 10 minutes | Cook time: 15 minutes | Serves 4

450 g boneless, skinless chicken tenderloins, cut into strips
3 bell peppers, any color, cut into chunks
1 onion, cut into chunks

1 tablespoon olive oil
1 tablespoon fajita seasoning mix
Cooking spray

Preheat the air fryer to 190ºC. In a large bowl, mix together the chicken, bell peppers, onion, olive oil, and fajita seasoning mix until completely coated. Spray the air fryer basket lightly with cooking spray. Place the chicken and vegetables in the air fryer basket and lightly spray with cooking spray. Air fry for 7 minutes. Shake the basket and air fry for an additional 5 to 8 minutes, until the chicken is cooked through and the veggies are starting to char. Serve warm.

Buttermilk Breaded Chicken

Prep time: 7 minutes | Cook time: 20 to 25 minutes | Serves 4

125 g all-purpose flour
2 teaspoons paprika
Pinch salt
Freshly ground black pepper, to taste
80 ml buttermilk
2 eggs

2 tablespoons extra-virgin olive oil
185 g bread crumbs
6 chicken pieces, drumsticks, breasts, and thighs, patted dry
Cooking oil spray

In a shallow bowl, stir together the flour, paprika, salt, and pepper. In another bowl, beat the buttermilk and eggs until smooth. In a third bowl, stir together the olive oil and bread crumbs until mixed.

Dredge the chicken in the flour, dip in the eggs to coat, and finally press into the bread crumbs, patting the crumbs firmly onto the chicken skin. Insert the crisper plate into the basket and the basket into the unit. Preheat the unit by selecting AIR FRY, setting the temperature to 190ºC, and setting the time to 3 minutes. Select START/STOP to begin. Once the unit is preheated, spray the crisper plate with cooking oil. Place the chicken into the basket. Select AIR FRY, set the temperature to 190ºC, and set the time to 25 minutes. Select START/STOP to begin. After 10 minutes, flip the chicken. Resume cooking. After 10 minutes more, check the chicken. If a food thermometer inserted into the chicken registers 76ºC and the chicken is brown and crisp, it is done. Otherwise, resume cooking for up to 5 minutes longer. When the cooking is complete, let cool for 5 minutes, then serve.

Crunchy Chicken Tenders

Prep time: 5 minutes | Cook time: 12 minutes | Serves 4

1 egg
60 ml unsweetened almond milk
30 g whole wheat flour
30 g whole wheat bread crumbs
½ teaspoon salt

½ teaspoon black pepper
½ teaspoon dried thyme
½ teaspoon dried sage
½ teaspoon garlic powder
450 g chicken tenderloins
1 lemon, quartered

Preheat the air fryer to 184ºC. In a shallow bowl, beat together the egg and almond milk until frothy. In a separate shallow bowl, whisk together the flour, bread crumbs, salt, pepper, thyme, sage, and garlic powder. Dip each chicken tenderloin into the egg mixture, then into the bread crumb mixture, coating the outside with the crumbs. Place the breaded chicken tenderloins into the bottom of the air fryer basket in an even layer, making sure that they don't touch each other. Cook for 6 minutes, then turn and cook for an additional 5 to 6 minutes. Serve with lemon slices.

Chipotle Aioli Wings

Prep time: 5 minutes | Cook time: 25 minutes | Serves 6

900 g bone-in chicken wings
½ teaspoon salt
¼ teaspoon ground black pepper

2 tablespoons mayonnaise
2 teaspoons chipotle powder
2 tablespoons lemon juice

In a large bowl, toss wings in salt and pepper, then place into ungreased air fryer basket. Adjust the temperature to 200ºC and air fry for 25 minutes, shaking the basket twice while cooking. Wings will be done when golden and have an internal temperature of at least 76ºC. In a small bowl, whisk together mayonnaise, chipotle powder, and lemon juice. Place cooked wings into a large serving bowl and drizzle with aioli. Toss to coat. Serve warm.

Ginger Turmeric Chicken Thighs

Prep time: 5 minutes | Cook time: 25 minutes | Serves 4

4 (115 g) boneless, skin-on chicken thighs	½ teaspoon salt
2 tablespoons coconut oil, melted	½ teaspoon garlic powder
½ teaspoon ground turmeric	½ teaspoon ground ginger
	¼ teaspoon ground black pepper

Place chicken thighs in a large bowl and drizzle with coconut oil. Sprinkle with remaining ingredients and toss to coat both sides of thighs. Place thighs skin side up into ungreased air fryer basket. Adjust the temperature to 200°C and air fry for 25 minutes. After 10 minutes, turn thighs. When 5 minutes remain, flip thighs once more. Chicken will be done when skin is golden brown and the internal temperature is at least 76°C. Serve warm.

Almond-Crusted Chicken

Prep time: 15 minutes | Cook time: 25 minutes | Serves 4

20 g slivered almonds	2 tablespoons full-fat mayonnaise
2 (170 g) boneless, skinless chicken breasts	1 tablespoon Dijon mustard

Pulse the almonds in a food processor or chop until finely chopped. Place almonds evenly on a plate and set aside. Completely slice each chicken breast in half lengthwise. Mix the mayonnaise and mustard in a small bowl and then coat chicken with the mixture. Lay each piece of chicken in the chopped almonds to fully coat. Carefully move the pieces into the air fryer basket. Adjust the temperature to 180°C and air fry for 25 minutes. Chicken will be done when it has reached an internal temperature of 76°C or more. Serve warm.

Chicken Enchiladas

Prep time: 10 minutes | Cook time: 8 minutes | Serves 4

Oil, for spraying	and drained
420 g shredded cooked chicken	1 (115 g) can diced green chilies, drained
1 package taco seasoning	
8 flour tortillas, at room temperature	1 (280 g) can red or green enchilada sauce
60 g canned black beans, rinsed	235 g shredded Cheddar cheese

Line the air fryer basket with parchment and spray lightly with oil. (Do not skip the step of lining the basket; the parchment will keep the sauce and cheese from dripping through the holes.) In a small bowl, mix together the chicken and taco seasoning. Divide the mixture among the tortillas. Top with the black beans and green chilis. Carefully roll up each tortilla. Place the enchiladas, seam-side down, in the prepared basket. You may need to work in batches, depending on the size of your air fryer. Spoon the enchilada sauce over the enchiladas. Use just enough sauce to keep them from drying out. You can add more sauce when serving. Sprinkle the cheese on top. Air fry at 180°C for 5 to 8 minutes, or until heated through and the cheese is melted. Place 2 enchiladas on each plate and top with more enchilada sauce, if desired.

Chicken with Lettuce

Prep time: 15 minutes | Cook time: 14 minutes | Serves 4

450 g chicken breast tenders, chopped into bite-size pieces	1 tablespoon olive oil
½ onion, thinly sliced	1 tablespoon fajita seasoning
½ red bell pepper, seeded and thinly sliced	1 teaspoon kosher salt
	Juice of ½ lime
½ green bell pepper, seeded and thinly sliced	8 large lettuce leaves
	230 g prepared guacamole

Preheat the air fryer to 200°C. In a large bowl, combine the chicken, onion, and peppers. Drizzle with the olive oil and toss until thoroughly coated. Add the fajita seasoning and salt and toss again. Working in batches if necessary, arrange the chicken and vegetables in a single layer in the air fryer basket. Pausing halfway through the cooking time to shake the basket, air fry for 14 minutes, or until the vegetables are tender and a thermometer inserted into the thickest piece of chicken registers 76°C. Transfer the mixture to a serving platter and drizzle with the fresh lime juice. Serve with the lettuce leaves and top with the guacamole.

Garlic Soy Chicken Thighs

Prep time: 10 minutes | Cook time: 30 minutes | Serves 1 to 2

2 tablespoons chicken stock	2 large spring onions, cut into 2- to 3-inch batons, plus more, thinly sliced, for garnish
2 tablespoons reduced-sodium soy sauce	
1½ tablespoons sugar	2 bone-in, skin-on chicken thighs (198 to 225 g each)
4 garlic cloves, smashed and peeled	

Preheat the air fryer to 190°C. In a metal cake pan, combine the chicken stock, soy sauce, and sugar and stir until the sugar dissolves. Add the garlic cloves, spring onions, and chicken thighs, turning the thighs to coat them in the marinade, then resting them skin-side up. Place the pan in the air fryer and bake, flipping the thighs every 5 minutes after the first 10 minutes, until the chicken is cooked through and the marinade is reduced to a sticky glaze over the chicken, about 30 minutes. Remove the pan from the air fryer and serve the chicken thighs warm, with any remaining glaze spooned over top and sprinkled with more sliced spring onions.

Korean Honey Wings

Prep time: 10 minutes | Cook time: 25 minutes per batch | Serves 4

55 g gochujang, or red pepper paste	2 teaspoons ground ginger
55 g mayonnaise	1.4 kg whole chicken wings
2 tablespoons honey	Olive oil spray
1 tablespoon sesame oil	1 teaspoon salt
2 teaspoons minced garlic	½ teaspoon freshly ground
1 tablespoon sugar	black pepper

In a large bowl, whisk the gochujang, mayonnaise, honey, sesame oil, garlic, sugar, and ginger. Set aside. Insert the crisper plate into the basket and the basket into the unit. Preheat the unit by selecting AIR FRY, setting the temperature to 200ºC, and setting the time to 3 minutes. Select START/STOP to begin. To prepare the chicken wings, cut the wings in half. The meatier part is the drumette. Cut off and discard the wing tip from the flat part (or save the wing tips in the freezer to make chicken stock). Once the unit is preheated, spray the crisper plate with olive oil. Working in batches, place half the chicken wings into the basket, spray them with olive oil, and sprinkle with the salt and pepper. Select AIR FRY, set the temperature to 200ºC, and set the time to 20 minutes. Select START/STOP to begin. After 10 minutes, remove the basket, flip the wings, and spray them with more olive oil. Reinsert the basket to resume cooking. Cook the wings to an internal temperature of 76ºC, then transfer them to the bowl with the prepared sauce and toss to coat. Repeat steps 4, 5, 6, and 7 for the remaining chicken wings. Return the coated wings to the basket and air fry for 4 to 6 minutes more until the sauce has glazed the wings and the chicken is crisp. After 3 minutes, check the wings to make sure they aren't burning. Serve hot.

Chicken Thighs in Waffles

Prep time: 1 hour 20 minutes | Cook time: 40 minutes | Serves 4

For the chicken:	Cooking spray
4 chicken thighs, skin on	For the waffles:
240 ml low-fat buttermilk	65 g all-purpose flour
65 g all-purpose flour	65 g whole wheat pastry flour
½ teaspoon garlic powder	1 large egg, beaten
½ teaspoon mustard powder	240 ml low-fat buttermilk
1 teaspoon kosher salt	1 teaspoon baking powder
½ teaspoon freshly ground	2 tablespoons rapeseed oil
black pepper	½ teaspoon kosher salt
85 g honey, for serving	1 tablespoon granulated sugar

Combine the chicken thighs with buttermilk in a large bowl. Wrap the bowl in plastic and refrigerate to marinate for at least an hour. Preheat the air fryer to 180ºC. Spritz the air fryer basket with cooking spray. Combine the flour, mustard powder, garlic powder, salt, and black pepper in a shallow dish. Stir to mix well. Remove the thighs from the buttermilk and pat dry with paper towels. Sit the bowl of buttermilk aside. Dip the thighs in the flour mixture first, then into the buttermilk, and then into the flour mixture. Shake the excess off. Arrange 2 thighs in the preheated air fryer and spritz with cooking spray. Air fryer for 20 minutes or until an instant-read thermometer inserted in the thickest part of the chicken thighs registers at least 76ºC. Flip the thighs halfway through. Repeat with remaining thighs. Meanwhile, make the waffles: combine the ingredients for the waffles in a large bowl. Stir to mix well, then arrange the mixture in a waffle iron and cook until a golden and fragrant waffle forms. Remove the waffles from the waffle iron and slice into 4 pieces. Remove the chicken thighs from the air fryer and allow to cool for 5 minutes. Arrange each chicken thigh on each waffle piece and drizzle with 1 tablespoon of honey. Serve warm.

Coriander Chicken Kebabs

Prep time: 30 minutes | Cook time: 10 minutes | Serves 4

Chutney:	chopped
40 g unsweetened shredded coconut	1 jalapeño, seeded and roughly chopped
120 ml hot water	60-75 ml water, as needed
40 g fresh coriander leaves, roughly chopped	Juice of 1 lemon
	Chicken:
10 g fresh mint leaves, roughly chopped	450 g boneless, skinless chicken thighs, cut crosswise into thirds
6 cloves garlic, roughly	Olive oil spray

For the chutney: In a blender or food processor, combine the coconut and hot water; set aside to soak for 5 minutes. To the processor, add the coriander, mint, garlic, and jalapeño, along with 60 ml water. Blend at low speed, stopping occasionally to scrape down the sides. Add the lemon juice. With the blender or processor running, add only enough additional water to keep the contents moving. Turn the blender to high once the contents are moving freely and blend until the mixture is puréed. For the chicken: Place the chicken pieces in a large bowl. Add ¼ cup of the chutney and mix well to coat. Set aside the remaining chutney to use as a dip. Marinate the chicken for 15 minutes at room temperature. Spray the air fryer basket with olive oil spray. Arrange the chicken in the air fryer basket. Set the air fryer to 180ºC for 10 minutes. Use a meat thermometer to ensure that the chicken has reached an internal temperature of 76ºC. Serve the chicken with the remaining chutney.

Herb-Buttermilk Chicken Breast

Prep time: 5 minutes | Cook time: 40 minutes |
Serves 2

1 large bone-in, skin-on chicken breast	½ teaspoon dried dill
240 ml buttermilk	½ teaspoon onion powder
1½ teaspoons dried parsley	¼ teaspoon garlic powder
1½ teaspoons dried chives	¼ teaspoon dried tarragon
¾ teaspoon kosher salt	Cooking spray

Place the chicken breast in a bowl and pour over the buttermilk, turning the chicken in it to make sure it's completely covered. Let the chicken stand at room temperature for at least 20 minutes or in the refrigerator for up to 4 hours. Meanwhile, in a bowl, stir together the parsley, chives, salt, dill, onion powder, garlic powder, and tarragon. Preheat the air fryer to 150°C. Remove the chicken from the buttermilk, letting the excess drip off, then place the chicken skin-side up directly in the air fryer. Sprinkle the seasoning mix all over the top of the chicken breast, then let stand until the herb mix soaks into the buttermilk, at least 5 minutes. Spray the top of the chicken with cooking spray. Bake for 10 minutes, then increase the temperature to 180°C and bake until an instant-read thermometer inserted into the thickest part of the breast reads 80°C and the chicken is deep golden brown, 30 to 35 minutes. Transfer the chicken breast to a cutting board, let rest for 10 minutes, then cut the meat off the bone and cut into thick slices for serving.

Fried Chicken Breasts

Prep time: 30 minutes | Cook time: 12 to 14 minutes
| Serves 4

450 g boneless, skinless chicken breasts	cheese
180 ml dill pickle juice	½ teaspoon sea salt
70 g finely ground blanched almond flour	½ teaspoon freshly ground black pepper
70 g finely grated Parmesan	2 large eggs
	Avocado oil spray

Place the chicken breasts in a zip-top bag or between two pieces of plastic wrap. Using a meat mallet or heavy skillet, pound the chicken to a uniform ½-inch thickness. Place the chicken in a large bowl with the pickle juice. Cover and allow to brine in the refrigerator for up to 2 hours. In a shallow dish, combine the almond flour, Parmesan cheese, salt, and pepper. In a separate, shallow bowl, beat the eggs. Drain the chicken and pat it dry with paper towels. Dip in the eggs and then in the flour mixture, making sure to press the coating into the chicken. Spray both sides of the coated breasts with oil. Spray the air fryer basket with oil and put the chicken inside. Set the temperature to 200°C and air fry for 6 to 7 minutes. Carefully flip the breasts with a spatula. Spray the breasts again with oil and continue cooking for 6 to 7 minutes more, until golden and crispy.

Golden Tenders

Prep time: 10 minutes | Cook time: 15 minutes |
Serves 4

120 g panko bread crumbs	black pepper
1 tablespoon paprika	16 chicken tenders
½ teaspoon salt	115 g mayonnaise
¼ teaspoon freshly ground	Olive oil spray

In a medium bowl, stir together the panko, paprika, salt, and pepper. In a large bowl, toss together the chicken tenders and mayonnaise to coat. Transfer the coated chicken pieces to the bowl of seasoned panko and dredge to coat thoroughly. Press the coating onto the chicken with your fingers. Insert the crisper plate into the basket and the basket into the unit. Preheat the unit by selecting AIR FRY, setting the temperature to 180°C, and setting the time to 3 minutes. Select START/STOP to begin. Once the unit is preheated, place a parchment paper liner into the basket. Place the chicken into the basket and spray it with olive oil. Select AIR FRY, set the temperature to 180°C, and set the time to 15 minutes. Select START/STOP to begin. When the cooking is complete, the tenders will be golden brown and a food thermometer inserted into the chicken should register 76°C. For more even browning, remove the basket halfway through cooking and flip the tenders. Give them an extra spray of olive oil and reinsert the basket to resume cooking. This ensures they are crispy and brown all over. When the cooking is complete, serve.

Chapter 8 Fish and Seafood

Parmesan-Crusted Hake with Garlic Sauce

Prep time: 5 minutes | Cook time: 10 minutes | Serves 3

Fish:
6 tablespoons mayonnaise
1 tablespoon fresh lime juice
1 teaspoon Dijon mustard
150 g grated Parmesan cheese
Salt, to taste
¼ teaspoon ground black pepper, or more to taste

3 hake fillets, patted dry
Nonstick cooking spray
Garlic Sauce:
60 ml plain Greek yogurt
2 tablespoons olive oil
2 cloves garlic, minced
½ teaspoon minced tarragon leaves

Preheat the air fryer to 202°C. Mix the mayo, lime juice, and mustard in a shallow bowl and whisk to combine. In another shallow bowl, stir together the grated Parmesan cheese, salt, and pepper. Dredge each fillet in the mayo mixture, then roll them in the cheese mixture until they are evenly coated on both sides. Spray the air fryer basket with nonstick cooking spray. Arrange the fillets in the basket and air fry for 10 minutes, or until the fish flakes easily with a fork. Flip the fillets halfway through the cooking time. Meanwhile, in a small bowl, whisk all the ingredients for the sauce until well incorporated. Serve the fish warm alongside the sauce.

Parmesan Fish Fillets

Prep time: 8 minutes | Cook time: 17 minutes | Serves 4

50 g grated Parmesan cheese
½ teaspoon fennel seed
½ teaspoon tarragon
⅓ teaspoon mixed peppercorns

2 eggs, beaten
4 (110 g) fish fillets, halved
2 tablespoons dry white wine
1 teaspoon seasoned salt

Preheat the air fryer to 174°C. Place the grated Parmesan cheese, fennel seed, tarragon, and mixed peppercorns in a food processor and pulse for about 20 seconds until well combined. Transfer the cheese mixture to a shallow dish. Place the beaten eggs in another shallow dish. Drizzle the dry white wine over the top of fish fillets. Dredge each fillet in the beaten eggs on both sides, shaking off any excess, then roll them in the cheese mixture until fully coated. Season with the salt. Arrange the fillets in the air fryer basket and air fry for about 17 minutes, or until the fish is cooked through and no longer translucent. Flip the fillets once halfway through the cooking time. Cool for 5 minutes before serving.

Tuna Cakes

Prep time: 10 minutes | Cook time: 10 minutes | Serves 4

4 (85 g) tuna fillets, drained
1 large egg, whisked
2 tablespoons peeled and

chopped white onion
½ teaspoon Old Bay seasoning

In a large bowl, mix all ingredients together and form into four patties. Place patties into ungreased air fryer basket. Adjust the temperature to 204°C and air fry for 10 minutes. Patties will be browned and crispy when done. Let cool 5 minutes before serving.

Sole and Asparagus Bundles

Prep time: 10 minutes | Cook time: 14 minutes | Serves 2

230 g asparagus, trimmed
1 teaspoon extra-virgin olive oil, divided
Salt and pepper, to taste
4 (85 g) skinless sole fillets, ⅛ to ¼ inch thick
4 tablespoons unsalted butter,

softened
1 small shallot, minced
1 tablespoon chopped fresh tarragon
¼ teaspoon lemon zest plus ½ teaspoon juice
Vegetable oil spray

Preheat the air fryer to 150°C. Toss asparagus with ½ teaspoon oil, pinch salt, and pinch pepper in a bowl. Cover and microwave until bright green and just tender, about 3 minutes, tossing halfway through microwaving. Uncover and set aside to cool slightly. Make foil sling for air fryer basket by folding 1 long sheet of aluminum foil so it is 4 inches wide. Lay sheet of foil widthwise across basket, pressing foil into and up sides of basket. Fold excess foil as needed so that edges of foil are flush with top of basket. Lightly spray foil and basket with vegetable oil spray. Pat sole dry with paper towels and season with salt and pepper. Arrange fillets skinned side up on cutting board, with thicker ends closest to you. Arrange asparagus evenly across base of each fillet, then tightly roll fillets away from you around asparagus to form tidy bundles. Rub bundles evenly with remaining ½ teaspoon oil and arrange seam side down on sling in prepared basket. Bake until asparagus is tender and sole flakes apart when gently prodded with a paring knife, 14 to 18 minutes, using a sling to rotate bundles halfway through cooking. Combine butter, shallot, tarragon, and lemon zest and juice in a bowl. Using sling, carefully remove sole bundles from air fryer and transfer to individual plates. Top evenly with butter mixture and serve.

Savory Prawns

Prep time: 5 minutes | Cook time: 8 to 10 minutes | Serves 4

455 g fresh large prawns, peeled and deveined
1 tablespoon avocado oil
2 teaspoons minced garlic, divided
½ teaspoon red pepper flakes

Sea salt and freshly ground black pepper, to taste
2 tablespoons unsalted butter, melted
2 tablespoons chopped fresh parsley

Place the prawns in a large bowl and toss with the avocado oil, 1 teaspoon of minced garlic, and red pepper flakes. Season with salt and pepper. Set the air fryer to 176°C. Arrange the prawns in a single layer in the air fryer basket, working in batches if necessary. Cook for 6 minutes. Flip the prawns and cook for 2 to 4 minutes more, until the internal temperature of the prawns reaches 50°C. (The time it takes to cook will depend on the size of the prawns.) While the prawns are cooking, melt the butter in a small saucepan over medium heat and stir in the remaining 1 teaspoon of garlic. Transfer the cooked prawns to a large bowl, add the garlic butter, and toss well. Top with the parsley and serve warm.

Quick Prawns Skewers

Prep time: 10 minutes | Cook time: 5 minutes | Serves 5

1.8kg prawns, peeled and deveined
1 tablespoon dried rosemary

1 tablespoon avocado oil
1 teaspoon apple cider vinegar

Mix the prawns with dried rosemary, avocado oil, and apple cider vinegar. Then thread the prawns onto skewers and put in the air fryer. Cook the prawns at 204°C for 5 minutes.

Mediterranean-Style Cod

Prep time: 5 minutes | Cook time: 12 minutes | Serves 4

4 cod fillets, 170 g each
3 tablespoons fresh lemon juice
1 tablespoon olive oil
¼ teaspoon salt

6 cherry tomatoes, halved
45 g pitted and sliced kalamata olives

Place cod into an ungreased round nonstick baking dish. Pour lemon juice into dish and drizzle cod with olive oil. Sprinkle with salt. Place tomatoes and olives around baking dish in between fillets. Place dish into air fryer basket. Adjust the temperature to 176°C and bake for 12 minutes, carefully turning cod halfway through cooking. Fillets will be lightly browned, easily flake, and have an internal temperature of at least 64°C when done. Serve warm.

Tilapia Almondine

Prep time: 10 minutes | Cook time: 10 minutes | Serves 2

50 g almond flour or fine dried bread crumbs
2 tablespoons salted butter or ghee, melted
1 teaspoon black pepper
½ teaspoon kosher or coarse sea

salt
60 g mayonnaise
2 tilapia fillets
435 g thinly sliced almonds
Vegetable oil spray

In a small bowl, mix together the almond flour, butter, pepper and salt. Spread the mayonnaise on both sides of each fish fillet. Dredge the fillets in the almond flour mixture. Spread the sliced almonds on one side of each fillet, pressing lightly to adhere. Spray the air fryer basket with vegetable oil spray. Place the fish fillets in the basket. Set the air fryer to 164°C for 10 minutes, or until the fish flakes easily with a fork.

Foil-Packet Lobster Tail

Prep time: 15 minutes | Cook time: 12 minutes | Serves 2

2 lobster tails, 170 g each halved
2 tablespoons salted butter, melted

½ teaspoon Old Bay seasoning
Juice of ½ medium lemon
1 teaspoon dried parsley

Place the two halved tails on a sheet of aluminum foil. Drizzle with butter, Old Bay seasoning, and lemon juice. Seal the foil packets, completely covering tails. Place into the air fryer basket. Adjust the temperature to 192°C and air fry for 12 minutes. Once done, sprinkle with dried parsley and serve immediately.

Sea Bass with Roasted Root Vegetables

Prep time: 10 minutes | Cook time: 15 minutes | Serves 4

1 carrot, diced small
1 parsnip, diced small
1 swede, diced small
60 ml olive oil
1 teaspoon salt, divided

4 sea bass fillets
½ teaspoon onion powder
2 garlic cloves, minced
1 lemon, sliced, plus additional wedges for serving

Preheat the air fryer to 192°C. In a small bowl, toss the carrot, parsnip, and swede with olive oil and 1 teaspoon salt. Lightly season the sea bass with the remaining 1 teaspoon of salt and the onion powder, then place it into the air fryer basket in a single layer. Spread the garlic over the top of each fillet, then cover with lemon slices. Pour the prepared vegetables into the basket around and on top of the fish. Roast for 15 minutes. Serve with additional lemon wedges if desired.

Tuna Nuggets in Hoisin Sauce

Prep time: 15 minutes | Cook time: 5 to 7 minutes | Serves 4

120 ml hoisin sauce	½ small onion, quartered and
2 tablespoons rice wine vinegar	thinly sliced
2 teaspoons sesame oil	230 g fresh tuna, cut into 1-inch
1 teaspoon garlic powder	cubes
2 teaspoons dried lemongrass	Cooking spray
¼ teaspoon red pepper flakes	560 g cooked jasmine rice

Mix the hoisin sauce, vinegar, sesame oil, and seasonings together. Stir in the onions and tuna nuggets. Spray a baking pan with nonstick spray and pour in tuna mixture. Roast at 200°C for 3 minutes. Stir gently. Cook 2 minutes and stir again, checking for doneness. Tuna should be barely cooked through, just beginning to flake and still very moist. If necessary, continue cooking and stirring in 1-minute intervals until done. Serve warm over hot jasmine rice.

Almond Pesto Salmon

Prep time: 5 minutes | Cook time: 12 minutes | Serves 2

60 g pesto	(about 110 g each)
20 g sliced almonds, roughly	2 tablespoons unsalted butter,
chopped	melted
2 (1½-inch-thick) salmon fillets	

In a small bowl, mix pesto and almonds. Set aside. Place fillets into a round baking dish. Brush each fillet with butter and place half of the pesto mixture on the top of each fillet. Place dish into the air fryer basket. Adjust the temperature to 200°C and set the timer for 12 minutes. Salmon will easily flake when fully cooked and reach an internal temperature of at least 64°C. Serve warm.

Pecan-Crusted Tilapia

Prep time: 10minutes | Cook time: 10 minutes | Serves 4

160 g pecans	tablespoons water
45 g panko bread crumbs	4 tilapia fillets, 170g each
70 g plain flour	Vegetable oil, for spraying
2 tablespoons Cajun seasoning	Lemon wedges, for serving
2 eggs, beaten with 2	

Grind the pecans in the food processor until they resemble coarse meal. Combine the ground pecans with the panko on a plate. On a second plate, combine the flour and Cajun seasoning. Dry the tilapia fillets using paper towels and dredge them in the flour mixture, shaking off any excess. Dip the fillets in the egg mixture and then dredge them in the pecan and panko mixture, pressing the coating onto the fillets. Place the breaded fillets on a plate or rack. Preheat the air fryer to 192°C. Spray both sides of the breaded fillets with oil. Carefully transfer 2 of the fillets to the air fryer basket and air fry for 9 to 10 minutes, flipping once halfway through, until the flesh is opaque and flaky. Repeat with the remaining fillets. Serve immediately with lemon wedges.

Sole Fillets

Prep time: 10 minutes | Cook time: 5 to 8 minutes | Serves 4

1 egg white	4 sole fillets, 110 g each
1 tablespoon water	Salt and pepper, to taste
60 g panko breadcrumbs	Olive or vegetable oil for
2 tablespoons extra-light virgin	misting or cooking spray
olive oil	

Preheat the air fryer to 390°F (200°C). Beat together egg white and water in shallow dish. In another shallow dish, mix panko crumbs and oil until well combined and crumbly (best done by hand). Season sole fillets with salt and pepper to taste. Dip each fillet into egg mixture and then roll in panko crumbs, pressing in crumbs so that fish is nicely coated. Spray the air fryer basket with nonstick cooking spray and add fillets. Air fry at 200°C for 3 minutes. Spray fish fillets but do not turn. Cook 2 to 5 minutes longer or until golden brown and crispy. Using a spatula, carefully remove fish from basket and serve.

Prawn Creole Casserole

Prep time: 20 minutes | Cook time: 25 minutes | Serves 4

360 g prawns, peeled and	1 tablespoon cornflour
deveined	1 teaspoon Creole seasoning
50 g chopped celery	¾ teaspoon salt
50 g chopped onion	½ teaspoon freshly ground
50 g chopped green bell pepper	black pepper
2 large eggs, beaten	120 g shredded Cheddar cheese
240 ml single cream	Cooking spray
1 tablespoon butter, melted	

In a medium bowl, stir together the prawns, celery, onion, and green pepper. In another medium bowl, whisk the eggs, single cream, butter, cornflour, Creole seasoning, salt, and pepper until blended. Stir the egg mixture into the prawn mixture. Add the cheese and stir to combine. Preheat the air fryer to 150°C. Spritz a baking pan with oil. Transfer the prawn mixture to the prepared pan and place it in the air fryer basket. Bake for 25 minutes, stirring every 10 minutes, until a knife inserted into the center comes out clean. Serve immediately.

Prawn Kebabs

Prep time: 15 minutes | Cook time: 6 minutes | Serves 4

Olive or vegetable oil, for spraying

455 g medium raw prawns, peeled and deveined

4 tablespoons unsalted butter, melted

1 tablespoon Old Bay seasoning

1 tablespoon packed light brown sugar

1 teaspoon granulated garlic

1 teaspoon onion powder

½ teaspoon freshly ground black pepper

Line the air fryer basket with baking paper and spray lightly with oil. Thread the prawns onto the skewers and place them in the prepared basket. In a small bowl, mix together the butter, Old Bay, brown sugar, garlic, onion powder, and black pepper. Brush the sauce on the prawns. Air fry at 204°C for 5 to 6 minutes, or until pink and firm. Serve immediately.

Scallops in Lemon-Butter Sauce

Prep time: 10 minutes | Cook time: 6 minutes | Serves 2

8 large dry sea scallops (about 340 g)

Salt and freshly ground black pepper, to taste

2 tablespoons olive oil

2 tablespoons unsalted butter, melted

2 tablespoons chopped flat-leaf parsley

1 tablespoon fresh lemon juice

2 teaspoons capers, drained and chopped

1 teaspoon grated lemon zest

1 clove garlic, minced

Preheat the air fryer to 204°C. Use a paper towel to pat the scallops dry. Sprinkle lightly with salt and pepper. Brush with the olive oil. Arrange the scallops in a single layer in the air fryer basket. Pausing halfway through the cooking time to turn the scallops, air fry for about 6 minutes until firm and opaque. Meanwhile, in a small bowl, combine the oil, butter, parsley, lemon juice, capers, lemon zest, and garlic. Drizzle over the scallops just before serving.

Prawn Bake

Prep time: 15 minutes | Cook time: 5 minutes | Serves 4

400 g prawns, peeled and deveined

1 egg, beaten

120 ml coconut milk

120 g Cheddar cheese, shredded

½ teaspoon coconut oil

1 teaspoon ground coriander

In the mixing bowl, mix prawns with egg, coconut milk, Cheddar cheese, coconut oil, and ground coriander. Then put the mixture in the baking ramekins and put in the air fryer. Cook the prawns at 204°C for 5 minutes.

Honey-Glazed Salmon

Prep time: 5 minutes | Cook time: 12 minutes | Serves 4

60 ml raw honey

4 garlic cloves, minced

1 tablespoon olive oil

½ teaspoon salt

Olive oil cooking spray

4 (1½-inch-thick) salmon fillets

Preheat the air fryer to 192°C. In a small bowl, mix together the honey, garlic, olive oil, and salt. Spray the bottom of the air fryer basket with olive oil cooking spray, and place the salmon in a single layer on the bottom of the air fryer basket. Brush the top of each fillet with the honey-garlic mixture, and roast for 10 to 12 minutes, or until the internal temperature reaches 64°C.

Tilapia with Pecans

Prep time: 20 minutes | Cook time: 16 minutes | Serves 5

2 tablespoons ground flaxseeds

1 teaspoon paprika

Sea salt and white pepper, to taste

1 teaspoon garlic paste

2 tablespoons extra-virgin olive oil

65 g pecans, ground

5 tilapia fillets, sliced into halves

Combine the ground flaxseeds, paprika, salt, white pepper, garlic paste, olive oil, and ground pecans in a sealable freezer bag. Add the fish fillets and shake to coat well. Spritz the air fryer basket with cooking spray. Cook in the preheated air fryer at 204°C for 10 minutes; turn them over and cook for 6 minutes more. Work in batches. Serve with lemon wedges, if desired. Enjoy!

Easy Scallops

Prep time: 5 minutes | Cook time: 4 minutes | Serves 2

12 medium sea scallops, rinsed and patted dry

1 teaspoon fine sea salt

¾ teaspoon ground black

pepper, plus more for garnish

Fresh thyme leaves, for garnish (optional)

Avocado oil spray

Preheat the air fryer to 200°C. Coat the air fryer basket with avocado oil spray. Place the scallops in a medium bowl and spritz with avocado oil spray. Sprinkle the salt and pepper to season. Transfer the seasoned scallops to the air fryer basket, spacing them apart. You may need to work in batches to avoid overcrowding. Air fry for 4 minutes, flipping the scallops halfway through, or until the scallops are firm and reach an internal temperature of just 64°C on a meat thermometer. Remove from the basket and repeat with the remaining scallops. Sprinkle the pepper and thyme leaves on top for garnish, if desired. Serve immediately.

chilli Tilapia

Prep time: 5 minutes | Cook time: 20 minutes | Serves 4

4 tilapia fillets, boneless
1 teaspoon chilli flakes
1 teaspoon dried oregano

1 tablespoon avocado oil
1 teaspoon mustard

Rub the tilapia fillets with chilli flakes, dried oregano, avocado oil, and mustard and put in the air fryer. Cook it for 10 minutes per side at 182°C.

Golden Prawns

Prep time: 20 minutes | Cook time: 7 minutes | Serves 4

2 egg whites
60 g coconut flour
120 g Parmigiano-Reggiano, grated
½ teaspoon celery seeds
½ teaspoon porcini powder
½ teaspoon onion powder

1 teaspoon garlic powder
½ teaspoon dried rosemary
½ teaspoon sea salt
½ teaspoon ground black pepper
680 g prawns, peeled and deveined

Whisk the egg with coconut flour and Parmigiano-Reggiano. Add in seasonings and mix to combine well. Dip your prawns in the batter. Roll until they are covered on all sides. Cook in the preheated air fryer at 200°C for 5 to 7 minutes or until golden brown. Work in batches. Serve with lemon wedges if desired.

Garlic Prawns

Prep time: 15 minutes | Cook time: 10 minutes | Serves 3

Prawns:
Olive or vegetable oil, for spraying
450 g medium raw prawns, peeled and deveined
6 tablespoons unsalted butter, melted
120 g panko bread crumbs
2 tablespoons garlic granules

1 teaspoon salt
½ teaspoon freshly ground black pepper
Garlic Butter Sauce:
115 g unsalted butter
2 teaspoons garlic granules
¾ teaspoon salt (omit if using salted butter)

Make the Prawns Preheat the air fryer to 204°C. Line the air fryer basket with baking paper and spray lightly with oil. Place the prawns and melted butter in a zip-top plastic bag, seal, and shake well, until evenly coated. In a medium bowl, mix together the breadcrumbs, garlic, salt, and black pepper. Add the prawns to the panko mixture and toss until evenly coated. Shake off any excess coating. Place the prawns in the prepared basket and spray lightly with oil. Cook for 8 to 10 minutes, flipping and spraying with oil after 4 to 5 minutes, until golden brown and crispy. Make the Garlic Butter Sauce In a microwave-safe bowl, combine the butter, garlic, and salt and microwave on 50% power for 30 to 60 seconds, stirring every 15 seconds, until completely melted. Serve the prawns immediately with the garlic butter sauce on the side for dipping.

Jalea

Prep time: 20 minutes | Cook time: 10 minutes | Serves 4

Salsa Criolla:
½ red onion, thinly sliced
2 tomatoes, diced
1 serrano or jalapeño pepper, deseeded and diced
1 clove garlic, minced
5 g chopped fresh coriander
Pinch of kosher or coarse sea salt
3 limes
Fried Seafood:
455 g firm, white-fleshed fish such as cod (add an extra 230 g fish if not using prawns)

20 large or jumbo prawns, peeled and deveined
30 g plain flour
40 g cornflour
1 teaspoon garlic powder
1 teaspoon kosher or coarse sea salt
¼ teaspoon cayenne pepper
240 g panko bread crumbs
2 eggs, beaten with 2 tablespoons water
Vegetable oil, for spraying
Mayonnaise or tartar sauce, for serving (optional)

To make the Salsa Criolla, combine the red onion, tomatoes, pepper, garlic, cilantro, and salt in a medium bowl. Add the juice and zest of 2 of the limes. Refrigerate the salad while you make the fish. To make the seafood, cut the fish fillets into strips approximately 2 inches long and 1 inch wide. Place the flour, cornstarch, garlic powder, salt, and cayenne pepper on a plate and whisk to combine. Place the panko on a separate plate. Dredge the fish strips in the seasoned flour mixture, shaking off any excess. Dip the strips in the egg mixture, coating them completely, then dredge in the panko, shaking off any excess. Place the fish strips on a plate or rack. Repeat with the prawns, if using. Spray the air fryer basket with oil, and preheat the air fryer to 204°C. Working in 2 or 3 batches, arrange the fish and prawns in a single layer in the basket, taking care not to crowd the basket. Spray with oil. Air fry for 5 minutes, then flip and air fry for another 4 to 5 minutes until the outside is brown and crisp and the inside of the fish is opaque and flakes easily with a fork. Repeat with the remaining seafood. Place the fried seafood on a platter. Use a slotted spoon to remove the salsa criolla from the bowl, leaving behind any liquid that has accumulated. Place the salsa criolla on top of the fried seafood. Serve immediately with the remaining lime, cut into wedges, and mayonnaise or tartar sauce as desired.

Chapter 9 Beef, Pork, and Lamb

Beef and Spinach Rolls

Prep time: 10 minutes | Cook time: 14 minutes | Serves 2

3 teaspoons pesto

900 g beef bavette or skirt steak

6 slices low-moisture Mozarella or other melting cheese

85 g roasted red peppers

180 ml baby spinach

1 teaspoon sea salt

1 teaspoon black pepper

Preheat the air fryer to 204°C. Spoon equal amounts of the pesto onto each steak and spread it across evenly. Put the cheese, roasted red peppers and spinach on top of the meat, about three-quarters of the way down. Roll the steak up, holding it in place with toothpicks. Sprinkle with the sea salt and pepper. Put inside the air fryer and air fry for 14 minutes, turning halfway through the cooking time. Allow the beef to rest for 10 minutes before slicing up and serving.

Steak, Broccoli, and Mushroom Rice Bowls

Prep time: 10 minutes | Cook time: 15 to 18 minutes | Serves 4

2 tablespoons cornflour

120 ml low-sodium beef stock

1 teaspoon reduced-salt soy sauce

340 g rump steak, cut into 1-inch cubes

120 ml broccoli florets

1 onion, chopped

235 ml sliced white or chestnut mushrooms

1 tablespoon grated peeled fresh ginger

Cooked brown rice (optional), for serving

In a medium bowl, stir together the cornflour, beef stock, and soy sauce until the cornflour is completely dissolved. Add the beef cubes and toss to coat. Let stand for 5 minutes at room temperature. Insert the crisper plate into the basket and the basket into the unit. Preheat the unit by selecting AIR FRY, setting the temperature to 204°C, and setting the time to 3 minutes. Select START/STOP to begin. Once the unit is preheated, use a slotted spoon to transfer the beef from the stock mixture into a medium metal bowl that fits into the basket. Reserve the stock. Add the broccoli, onion, mushrooms, and ginger to the beef. Place the bowl into the basket. Select AIR FRY, set the temperature to 204°C, and set the time to 18 minutes. Select START/STOP to begin. After about 12 minutes, check the beef and broccoli. If a food thermometer inserted into the beef registers at least 64°C and the vegetables are tender, add the reserved stock and resume cooking for about 3 minutes until the sauce boils. If not, resume cooking for about 3 minutes before

adding the reservedstock. When the cooking is complete, serve immediately over hot cooked brown rice, if desired.

Bacon-Wrapped Cheese Pork

Prep time: 10 minutes | Cook time: 20 minutes | Serves 4

4 (1-inch-thick) boneless pork chops

2 (150 g) packages Boursin

cheese

8 slices thin-cut bacon

Spray the air fryer basket with avocado oil. Preheat the air fryer to 204°C. Place one of the chops on a cutting board. With a sharp knife held parallel to the cutting board, make a 1-inch-wide incision on the top edge of the chop. Carefully cut into the chop to form a large pocket, leaving a ½-inch border along the sides and bottom. Repeat with the other 3 chops. Snip the corner of a large resealable plastic bag to form a ¾-inch hole. Place the Boursin cheese in the bag and pipe the cheese into the pockets in the chops, dividing the cheese evenly among them. Wrap 2 slices of bacon around each chop and secure the ends with toothpicks. Place the bacon-wrapped chops in the air fryer basket and cook for 10 minutes, then flip the chops and cook for another 8 to 10 minutes, until the bacon is crisp, the chops are cooked through, and the internal temperature reaches 64°C. Store leftovers in an airtight container in the refrigerator for up to 3 days. Reheat in a preheated 204°C air fryer for 5 minutes, or until warmed through.

Pork Loin Roast

Prep time: 30 minutes | Cook time: 55 minutes | Serves 6

680 g boneless pork loin joint, washed

1 teaspoon mustard seeds

1 teaspoon garlic powder

1 teaspoon porcini powder

1 teaspoon onion granules

¾ teaspoon sea salt flakes

1 teaspoon red pepper flakes, crushed

2 dried sprigs thyme, crushed

2 tablespoons lime juice

Firstly, score the meat using a small knife; make sure to not cut too deep. In a small-sized mixing dish, combine all seasonings in the order listed above; mix to combine well. Massage the spice mix into the pork meat to evenly distribute. Drizzle with lemon juice. Set the air fryer to 182°C. Place the pork in the air fryer basket; roast for 25 to 30 minutes. Pause the machine, check for doneness and cook for 25 minutes more.

Bacon-Wrapped Vegetable Kebabs

Prep time: 10 minutes | Cook time: 10 to 12 minutes | Serves 4

110 g mushrooms, sliced
1 small courgette, sliced
12 baby plum tomatoes
110 g sliced bacon, halved

Avocado oil spray
Sea salt and freshly ground
black pepper, to taste

Stack 3 mushroom slices, 1 courgette slice, and 1 tomato. Wrap a bacon strip around the vegetables and thread them onto a skewer. Repeat with the remaining vegetables and bacon. Spray with oil and sprinkle with salt and pepper. Set the air fryer to 204°C. Place the skewers in the air fryer basket in a single layer, working in batches if necessary, and air fry for 5 minutes. Flip the skewers and cook for 5 to 7 minutes more, until the bacon is crispy and the vegetables are tender. Serve warm.

Bacon and Cheese Stuffed Pork Chops

Prep time: 10 minutes | Cook time: 12 minutes | Serves 4

15 g plain pork scratchings,
finely crushed
120 ml shredded sharp Cheddar
cheese
4 slices cooked bacon,

crumbled
4 (110 g) boneless pork chops
½ teaspoon salt
¼ teaspoon ground black
pepper

In a small bowl, mix pork scratchings, Cheddar, and bacon. Make a 3-inch slit in the side of each pork chop and stuff with ¼ pork rind mixture. Sprinkle each side of pork chops with salt and pepper. Place pork chops into ungreased air fryer basket, stuffed side up. Adjust the temperature to 204°C and air fry for 12 minutes. Pork chops will be browned and have an internal temperature of at least 64°C when done. Serve warm.

Italian Sausage and Cheese Meatballs

Prep time: 10 minutes | Cook time: 20 minutes | Serves 4

230 g sausage meat with Italian
seasoning added to taste
230 g 85% lean beef mince
120 ml shredded sharp Cheddar

cheese
½ teaspoon onion granules
½ teaspoon garlic powder
½ teaspoon black pepper

In a large bowl, gently mix the sausage meat, beef mince, cheese, onion granules, garlic powder, and pepper until well combined. Form the mixture into 16 meatballs. Place the meatballs in a single layer in the air fryer basket. Set the air fryer to 176°C for 20 minutes, turning the meatballs halfway through the cooking time. Use a meat thermometer to ensure the meatballs have reached an internal temperature of 72°C (medium).

Lamb and Cucumber Burgers

Prep time: 8 minutes | Cook time: 15 to 18 minutes | Serves 4

1 teaspoon ground ginger
½ teaspoon ground coriander
¼ teaspoon freshly ground
white pepper
½ teaspoon ground cinnamon
½ teaspoon dried oregano
¼ teaspoon ground allspice
¼ teaspoon ground turmeric
120 ml low-fat plain Greek

yogurt
450 g lamb mince
1 teaspoon garlic paste
¼ teaspoon salt
¼ teaspoon freshly ground
black pepper
Cooking oil spray
4 hamburger buns
½ cucumber, thinly sliced

In a small bowl, stir together the ginger, coriander, white pepper, cinnamon, oregano, allspice, and turmeric. Put the yogurt in a small bowl and add half the spice mixture. Mix well and refrigerate. Insert the crisper plate into the basket and the basket into the unit. Preheat the unit by selecting AIR FRY, setting the temperature to 182°C, and setting the time to 3 minutes. Select START/STOP to begin. In a large bowl, combine the lamb, garlic paste, remaining spice mix, salt, and pepper. Gently but thoroughly mix the ingredients with your hands. Form the meat into 4 patties. Once the unit is preheated, spray the crisper plate with cooking oil, and place the patties into the basket. Select AIR FRY, set the temperature to 182°C, and set the time to 18 minutes. Select START/STOP to begin. After 15 minutes, check the burgers. If a food thermometer inserted into the burgers registers 72°C, the burgers are done. If not, resume cooking. When the cooking is complete, assemble the burgers on the buns with cucumber slices and a dollop of the yogurt dip.

Air Fried Crispy Venison

Prep time: 10 minutes | Cook time: 20 minutes | Serves 4

2 eggs
60 ml milk
235 ml whole wheat flour
½ teaspoon salt
¼ teaspoon ground black

pepper
450 g venison backstrap/
striploin, sliced
Cooking spray

Preheat the air fryer to 182°C and spritz with cooking spray. Whisk the eggs with milk in a large bowl. Combine the flour with salt and ground black pepper in a shallow dish. Dredge the venison in the flour first, then into the egg mixture. Shake the excess off and roll the venison back over the flour to coat well. Arrange half of the venison in the preheated air fryer and spritz with cooking spray. Air fry for 10 minutes or until the internal temperature of the venison reaches at least 64°C for medium rare. Flip the venison halfway through. Repeat with remaining venison. Serve immediately.

Pork Chops with Caramelized Onions

Prep time: 20 minutes | Cook time: 23 to 34 minutes | Serves 4

4 bone-in pork chops (230 g each)	divided
1 to 2 tablespoons oil	1 brown onion, thinly sliced
2 tablespoons Cajun seasoning,	1 green pepper, thinly sliced
	2 tablespoons light brown sugar

Spritz the pork chops with oil. Sprinkle 1 tablespoon of Cajun seasoning on one side of the chops. Preheat the air fryer to 204°C. Line the air fryer basket with parchment paper and spritz the parchment with oil. Place 2 pork chops, spice-side up, on the paper. Cook for 4 minutes. Flip the chops, sprinkle with the remaining 1 tablespoon of Cajun seasoning, and cook for 4 to 8 minutes more until the internal temperature reaches 64°C, depending on the chops' thickness. Remove and keep warm while you cook the remaining 2 chops. Set the chops aside. In a baking pan, combine the onion, pepper, and brown sugar, stirring until the vegetables are coated. Place the pan in the air fryer basket and cook for 4 minutes. Stir the vegetables. Cook for 3 to 6 minutes more to your desired doneness. Spoon the vegetable mixture over the chops to serve.

Sausage and Courgette Lasagna

Prep time: 25 minutes | Cook time: 56 minutes | Serves 4

1 courgette	180 ml ricotta cheese
Avocado oil spray	235 ml shredded gruyere
170 g hot Italian-seasoned	cheese, divided
sausage, casings removed	120 ml finely grated Parmesan
60 g mushrooms, stemmed and	cheese
sliced	Sea salt and freshly ground
1 teaspoon minced garlic	black pepper, to taste
235 ml keto-friendly marinara	Fresh basil, for garnish
sauce	

Cut the courgette into long thin slices using a mandoline slicer or sharp knife. Spray both sides of the slices with oil. Place the slices in a single layer in the air fryer basket, working in batches if necessary. Set the air fryer to 164°C and air fry for 4 to 6 minutes, until most of the moisture has been released from the courgette. Place a large skillet over medium-high heat. Crumble the sausage into the hot skillet and cook for 6 minutes, breaking apart the meat with the back of a spoon. Remove the sausage from the skillet, leaving any fats that remain. Add the mushrooms to the skillet and cook for 10 minutes, until the liquid nearly evaporates. Add the garlic and cook for 1 minute more. Stir in the marinara and cook for 2 more minutes. In a medium bowl, combine the ricotta cheese, 120 ml of gruyere cheese, Parmesan cheese, and salt and pepper to taste. Spread 60 ml of the meat sauce in the bottom of a deep pan (or other pan that fits inside your air fryer). Top with

half of the courgette slices. Add half of the cheese mixture. Top the cheese with half of the remaining meat sauce. Layer the remaining courgette over the meat sauce and top with the remaining cheese mixture. Top the lasagna with the remaining 120 ml of fontina cheese. Cover the lasagna with aluminum foil or parchment paper and place it in the air fryer. Bake for 25 minutes. Remove the foil and cook for 8 to 10 minutes more. Allow the lasagna to rest for 15 minutes before cutting and serving. Garnish with basil.

Kielbasa Sausage with Pineapple and Peppers

Prep time: 15 minutes | Cook time: 10 minutes | Serves 2 to 4

340 g kielbasa sausage, cut into	1 tablespoon barbecue
½-inch slices	seasoning
1 (230 g) can pineapple chunks	1 tablespoon soy sauce
in juice, drained	Cooking spray
235 ml pepper chunks	

Preheat the air fryer to 200°C. Spritz the air fryer basket with cooking spray. Combine all the ingredients in a large bowl. Toss to mix well. Pour the sausage mixture in the preheated air fryer. Air fry for 10 minutes or until the sausage is lightly browned and the pepper and pineapple are soft. Shake the basket halfway through. Serve immediately.

Vietnamese Grilled Pork

Prep time: 30 minutes | Cook time: 20 minutes | Serves 6

60 ml minced brown onion	½ teaspoon black pepper
2 tablespoons sugar	680 g boneless pork shoulder,
2 tablespoons vegetable oil	cut into ½-inch-thick slices
1 tablespoon minced garlic	60 ml chopped salted roasted
1 tablespoon fish sauce	peanuts
1 tablespoon minced fresh	2 tablespoons chopped fresh
lemongrass	coriander or parsley
2 teaspoons dark soy sauce	

In a large bowl, combine the onion, sugar, vegetable oil, garlic, fish sauce, lemongrass, soy sauce, and pepper. Add the pork and toss to coat. Marinate at room temperature for 30 minutes, or cover and refrigerate for up to 24 hours. Arrange the pork slices in the air fryer basket; discard the marinade. Set the air fryer to 204°C for 20 minutes, turning the pork halfway through the cooking time. Transfer the pork to a serving platter. Sprinkle with the peanuts and coriander and serve.

London Broil with Herb Butter

Prep time: 30 minutes | Cook time: 20 to 25 minutes | Serves 4

680 g bavette or skirt steak	softened
60 ml olive oil	1 tablespoon chopped fresh
2 tablespoons balsamic vinegar	parsley
1 tablespoon Worcestershire	¼ teaspoon salt
sauce	¼ teaspoon dried ground
4 cloves garlic, minced	rosemary or thyme
Herb Butter:	¼ teaspoon garlic powder
6 tablespoons unsalted butter,	Pinch of red pepper flakes

Place the beef in a gallon-size resealable bag. In a small bowl, whisk together the olive oil, balsamic vinegar, Worcestershire sauce, and garlic. Pour the marinade over the beef, massaging gently to coat, and seal the bag. Let sit at room temperature for an hour or refrigerate overnight. To make the herb butter: In a small bowl, mix the butter with the parsley, salt, rosemary, garlic powder, and red pepper flakes until smooth. Cover and refrigerate until ready to use. Preheat the air fryer to 204°C. Remove the beef from the marinade (discard the marinade) and place the beef in the air fryer basket. Pausing halfway through the cooking time to turn the meat, air fry for 20 to 25 minutes, until a thermometer inserted into the thickest part indicates the desired doneness, 52°C (rare) to 64°C (medium). Let the beef rest for 10 minutes before slicing. Serve topped with the herb butter.

Easy Beef Satay

Prep time: 30 minutes | Cook time: 8 minutes | Serves 4

450 g beef bavette or skirt	1 tablespoon minced garlic
steak, thinly sliced into long	1 tablespoon sugar
strips	1 teaspoon Sriracha or other hot
2 tablespoons vegetable oil	sauce
1 tablespoon fish sauce	1 teaspoon ground coriander
1 tablespoon soy sauce	120 ml chopped fresh coriander
1 tablespoon minced fresh	60 ml chopped roasted peanuts
ginger	

Place the beef strips in a large bowl or resealable plastic bag. Add the vegetable oil, fish sauce, soy sauce, ginger, garlic, sugar, Sriracha, coriander, and 60 ml of the fresh coriander to the bag. Seal and massage the bag to thoroughly coat and combine. Marinate at room temperature for 30 minutes, or cover and refrigerate for up to 24 hours. Using tongs, remove the beef strips from the bag and lay them flat in the air fryer basket, minimizing overlap as much as possible; discard the marinade. Set the air fryer to 204°C for 8 minutes, turning the beef strips halfway through the cooking time. Transfer the meat to a serving platter. Sprinkle with the remaining 60 ml coriander and the peanuts. Serve.

Broccoli and Pork Teriyaki

Prep time: 10 minutes | Cook time: 13 minutes | Serves 4

1 head broccoli, trimmed into	450 g pork tenderloin, trimmed
florets	and cut into 1-inch pieces
1 tablespoon extra-virgin olive	120 ml teriyaki sauce, divided
oil	Olive oil spray
¼ teaspoon sea salt	475 ml cooked brown rice
¼ teaspoon freshly ground	Sesame seeds, for garnish
black pepper	

Insert the crisper plate into the basket and the basket into the unit. Preheat the unit by selecting AIR ROAST, setting the temperature to 204°C, and setting the time to 3 minutes. Select START/STOP to begin. In a large bowl, toss together the broccoli, olive oil, salt, and pepper. In a medium bowl, toss together the pork and 3 tablespoons of teriyaki sauce to coat the meat. Once the unit is preheated, spray the crisper plate with olive oil. Put the broccoli and pork into the basket. Spray them with olive oil and drizzle with 1 tablespoon of teriyaki sauce. Select AIR ROAST, set the temperature to 204°C, and set the time to 13 minutes. Select START/STOP to begin. After 10 to 12 minutes, the broccoli is tender and light golden brown and a food thermometer inserted into the pork should register 64°C. Remove the basket and drizzle the broccoli and pork with the remaining 60 ml of teriyaki sauce and toss to coat. Reinsert the basket to resume cooking for 1 minute. When the cooking is complete, serve immediately over the hot cooked rice, if desired, garnished with the sesame seeds.

Sweet and Spicy Country-Style Ribs

Prep time: 10 minutes | Cook time: 25 minutes | Serves 4

2 tablespoons brown sugar	1 teaspoon coarse or flaky salt
2 tablespoons smoked paprika	1 teaspoon black pepper
1 teaspoon garlic powder	¼ to ½ teaspoon cayenne
1 teaspoon onion granules	pepper
1 teaspoon mustard powder	680 g boneless pork steaks
1 teaspoon ground cumin	235 ml barbecue sauce

In a small bowl, stir together the brown sugar, paprika, garlic powder, onion granules, mustard powder, cumin, salt, black pepper, and cayenne. Mix until well combined. Pat the ribs dry with a paper towel. Generously sprinkle the rub evenly over both sides of the ribs and rub in with your fingers. Place the ribs in the air fryer basket. Set the air fryer to 176°C for 15 minutes. Turn the ribs and brush with 120 ml of the barbecue sauce. Cook for an additional 10 minutes. Use a meat thermometer to ensure the pork has reached an internal temperature of 64°C. Serve with remaining barbecue sauce.

Beef Steak Fingers

Prep time: 5 minutes | Cook time: 8 minutes | Serves 4

4 small beef minute steaks	120 ml flour
Salt and ground black pepper, to taste	Cooking spray

Preheat the air fryer to 200°C. Cut minute steaks into 1-inch-wide strips. Sprinkle lightly with salt and pepper to taste. Roll in flour to coat all sides. Spritz air fryer basket with cooking spray. Put steak strips in air fryer basket in a single layer. Spritz top of steak strips with cooking spray. Air fry for 4 minutes, turn strips over, and spritz with cooking spray. Air fry 4 more minutes and test with fork for doneness. Steak fingers should be crispy outside with no red juices inside. Repeat steps 5 through 7 to air fry remaining strips. 1Serve immediately.

Swedish Meatloaf

Prep time: 10 minutes | Cook time: 35 minutes | Serves 8

680 g beef mince (85% lean)	Sauce:
110 g pork mince	120 ml (1 stick) unsalted butter
1 large egg (omit for egg-free)	120 ml shredded Swiss or mild
120 ml minced onions	Cheddar cheese (about 60 g)
60 ml tomato sauce	60 g cream cheese (60 ml),
2 tablespoons mustard powder	softened
2 cloves garlic, minced	80 ml beef stock
2 teaspoons fine sea salt	⅛ teaspoon ground nutmeg
1 teaspoon ground black pepper, plus more for garnish	Halved cherry tomatoes, for serving (optional)

Preheat the air fryer to 200°C. In a large bowl, combine the beef, pork, egg, onions, tomato sauce, mustard powder, garlic, salt, and pepper. Using your hands, mix until well combined. Place the meatloaf mixture in a loaf pan and place it in the air fryer. Bake for 35 minutes, or until cooked through and the internal temperature reaches 64°C. Check the meatloaf after 25 minutes; if it's getting too brown on the top, cover it loosely with foil to prevent burning. While the meatloaf cooks, make the sauce: Heat the butter in a saucepan over medium-high heat until it sizzles and brown flecks appear, stirring constantly to keep the butter from burning. Turn the heat down to low and whisk in the Swiss cheese, cream cheese, stock, and nutmeg. Simmer for at least 10 minutes. The longer it simmers, the more the flavors open up. When the meatloaf is done, transfer it to a serving tray and pour the sauce over it. Garnish with ground black pepper and serve with cherry tomatoes, if desired. Allow the meatloaf to rest for 10 minutes before slicing so it doesn't crumble apart. Store leftovers in an airtight container in the fridge for 3 days or in the freezer for up to a month. Reheat in a preheated 176°C air fryer for 4 minutes, or until heated through.

Reuben Beef Rolls with Thousand Island Sauce

Prep time: 15 minutes | Cook time: 10 minutes per batch | Makes 10 rolls

230 g cooked salt beef, chopped	Thousand Island Sauce:
120 ml drained and chopped sauerkraut	60 ml chopped dill pickles
1 (230 g) package cream cheese, softened	60 ml tomato ketchup
120 ml shredded Swiss cheese	180 ml mayonnaise
20 slices prosciutto	Fresh thyme leaves, for garnish
Cooking spray	2 tablespoons sugar
	⅛ teaspoon fine sea salt
	Ground black pepper, to taste

Preheat the air fryer to 204°C and spritz with cooking spray. Combine the beef, sauerkraut, cream cheese, and Swiss cheese in a large bowl. Stir to mix well. Unroll a slice of prosciutto on a clean work surface, then top with another slice of prosciutto crosswise. Scoop up 4 tablespoons of the beef mixture in the center. Fold the top slice sides over the filling as the ends of the roll, then roll up the long sides of the bottom prosciutto and make it into a roll shape. Overlap the sides by about 1 inch. Repeat with remaining filling and prosciutto. Arrange the rolls in the preheated air fryer, seam side down, and spritz with cooking spray. Air fry for 10 minutes or until golden and crispy. Flip the rolls halfway through. Work in batches to avoid overcrowding. Meanwhile, combine the ingredients for the sauce in a small bowl. Stir to mix well. Serve the rolls with the dipping sauce.

Cinnamon-Beef Kofta

Prep time: 10 minutes | Cook time: 13 minutes per batch | Makes 12 koftas

680 g lean beef mince	¾ teaspoon salt
1 teaspoon onion granules	¼ teaspoon cayenne
¾ teaspoon ground cinnamon	12 (3½- to 4-inch-long)
¾ teaspoon ground dried turmeric	cinnamon sticks
1 teaspoon ground cumin	Cooking spray

Preheat the air fryer to 192°C. Spritz the air fryer basket with cooking spray. Combine all the ingredients, except for the cinnamon sticks, in a large bowl. Toss to mix well. Divide and shape the mixture into 12 balls, then wrap each ball around each cinnamon stick and leave a quarter of the length uncovered. Arrange the beef-cinnamon sticks in the preheated air fryer and spritz with cooking spray. Work in batches to avoid overcrowding. Air fry for 13 minutes or until the beef is browned. Flip the sticks halfway through. Serve immediately.

Pepper Steak

Prep time: 30 minutes | Cook time: 16 to 20 minutes | Serves 4

450 g minute steak, cut into 1-inch pieces	black pepper
235 ml Italian dressing	60 ml cornflour
355 ml beef stock	235 ml thinly sliced pepper, any color
1 tablespoon soy sauce	235 ml chopped celery
½ teaspoon salt	1 tablespoon minced garlic
¼ teaspoon freshly ground	1 to 2 tablespoons oil

In a large resealable bag, combine the beef and Italian dressing. Seal the bag and refrigerate to marinate for 8 hours. In a small bowl, whisk the beef stock, soy sauce, salt, and pepper until blended. In another small bowl, whisk 60 ml water and the cornflour until dissolved. Stir the cornflour mixture into the beef stock mixture until blended. Preheat the air fryer to 192°C. Pour the stock mixture into a baking pan. Cook for 4 minutes. Stir and cook for 4 to 5 minutes more. Remove and set aside. Increase the air fryer temperature to 204°C. Line the air fryer basket with parchment paper. Remove the steak from the marinade and place it in a medium bowl. Discard the marinade. Stir in the pepper, celery, and garlic. Place the steak and pepper mixture on the parchment. Spritz with oil. Cook for 4 minutes. Shake the basket and cook for 4 to 7 minutes more, until the vegetables are tender and the meat reaches an internal temperature of 64°C. Serve with the gravy.

Beefy Poppers

Prep time: 15 minutes | Cook time: 15 minutes | Makes 8 poppers

8 medium jalapeño peppers, stemmed, halved, and seeded	1 teaspoon fine sea salt
1 (230 g) package cream cheese (or cream cheese style spread for dairy-free), softened	½ teaspoon ground black pepper
900 g beef mince (85% lean)	8 slices thin-cut bacon
	Fresh coriander leaves, for garnish

Spray the air fryer basket with avocado oil. Preheat the air fryer to 204°C. Stuff each jalapeño half with a few tablespoons of cream cheese. Place the halves back together again to form 8 jalapeños. Season the beef mince with the salt and pepper and mix with your hands to incorporate. Flatten about 110 g of beef in the palm of your hand and place a stuffed jalapeño in the center. Fold the beef around the jalapeño, forming an egg shape. Wrap the beef-covered jalapeño with a slice of bacon and secure it with a toothpick. Place the jalapeños in the air fryer basket, leaving space between them (if you're using a smaller air fryer, work in batches if necessary), and air fry for 15 minutes, or until the beef is cooked through and

the bacon is crispy. Garnish with coriander before serving. Store leftovers in an airtight container in the fridge for 3 days or in the freezer for up to a month. Reheat in a preheated 176°C air fryer for 4 minutes, or until heated through and the bacon is crispy.

Mexican Pork Chops

Prep time: 5 minutes | Cook time: 15 minutes | Serves 2

¼ teaspoon dried oregano	2 (110 g) boneless pork chops
1½ teaspoons taco seasoning or fajita seasoning mix	2 tablespoons unsalted butter, divided

Preheat the air fryer to 204°C. Combine the dried oregano and taco seasoning in a small bowl and rub the mixture into the pork chops. Brush the chops with 1 tablespoon butter. In the air fryer, air fry the chops for 15 minutes, turning them over halfway through to air fry on the other side. When the chops are a brown color, check the internal temperature has reached 64°C and remove from the air fryer. Serve with a garnish of remaining butter.

Cheesy Low-Carb Lasagna

Prep time: 10 minutes | Cook time: 10 minutes | Serves 4

Meat Layer:	230 g ricotta cheese
Extra-virgin olive oil	235 ml shredded Mozzarella cheese
450 g 85% lean beef mince	120 ml grated Parmesan cheese
235 ml marinara sauce	2 large eggs
60 ml diced celery	1 teaspoon dried Italian seasoning, crushed
60 ml diced red onion	½ teaspoon each minced garlic, garlic powder, and black pepper
½ teaspoon minced garlic	
Coarse or flaky salt and black pepper, to taste	
Cheese Layer:	

For the meat layer: Grease a cake pan with 1 teaspoon olive oil. In a large bowl, combine the beef mince, marinara, celery, onion, garlic, salt, and pepper. Place the seasoned meat in the pan. Place the pan in the air fryer basket. Set the air fryer to 192°C for 10 minutes. Meanwhile, for the cheese layer: In a medium bowl, combine the ricotta, half the Mozzarella, the Parmesan, lightly beaten eggs, Italian seasoning, minced garlic, garlic powder, and pepper. Stir until well blended. At the end of the cooking time, spread the cheese mixture over the meat mixture. Sprinkle with the remaining 120 ml Mozzarella. Set the air fryer to 192°C for 10 minutes, or until the cheese is browned and bubbling. At the end of the cooking time, use a meat thermometer to ensure the meat has reached an internal temperature of 72°C. Drain the fat and liquid from the pan. Let stand for 5 minutes before serving.

Blackened Steak Nuggets

Prep time: 10 minutes | Cook time: 7 minutes | Serves 2

450 g rib eye steak, cut into 1-inch cubes
2 tablespoons salted butter, melted
½ teaspoon paprika
½ teaspoon salt
¼ teaspoon garlic powder
¼ teaspoon onion granules
¼ teaspoon ground black pepper
⅛ teaspoon cayenne pepper

Place steak into a large bowl and pour in butter. Toss to coat. Sprinkle with remaining ingredients. Place bites into ungreased air fryer basket. Adjust the temperature to 204°C and air fry for 7 minutes, shaking the basket three times during cooking. Steak will be crispy on the outside and browned when done and internal temperature is at least 64°C for medium and 82°C for well-done. Serve warm.

Mustard Lamb Chops

Prep time: 5 minutes | Cook time: 14 minutes | Serves 4

Oil, for spraying
1 tablespoon Dijon mustard
2 teaspoons lemon juice
½ teaspoon dried tarragon
¼ teaspoon salt
¼ teaspoon freshly ground black pepper
4 (1¼-inch-thick) loin lamb chops

Preheat the air fryer to 200°C. Line the air fryer basket with parchment and spray lightly with oil. In a small bowl, mix together the mustard, lemon juice, tarragon, salt, and black pepper. Pat dry the lamb chops with a paper towel. Brush the chops on both sides with the mustard mixture. Place the chops in the prepared basket. You may need to work in batches, depending on the size of your air fryer. Cook for 8 minutes, flip, and cook for another 6 minutes, or until the internal temperature reaches 52°C for rare, 64°C for medium-rare, or 68°C for medium.

Fruited Ham

Prep time: 15 minutes | Cook time: 8 to 10 minutes | Serves 4

235 ml orange marmalade
60 ml packed light brown sugar
¼ teaspoon ground cloves
½ teaspoon mustard powder
1 to 2 tablespoons oil
450 g cooked ham, cut into 1-inch cubes
120 ml canned mandarin oranges, drained and chopped

In a small bowl, stir together the orange marmalade, brown sugar, cloves, and mustard powder until blended. Set aside. Preheat the air fryer to 160°C. Spritz a baking pan with oil. Place the ham cubes in the prepared pan. Pour the marmalade sauce over the ham to glaze it. Cook for 4 minutes. Stir and cook for 2 minutes more. Add the mandarin oranges and cook for 2 to 4 minutes more until the sauce begins to thicken and the ham is tender.

Parmesan-Crusted Pork Chops

Prep time: 5 minutes | Cook time: 12 minutes | Serves 4

1 large egg
120 ml grated Parmesan cheese
4 (110 g) boneless pork chops
½ teaspoon salt
¼ teaspoon ground black pepper

Whisk egg in a medium bowl and place Parmesan in a separate medium bowl. Sprinkle pork chops on both sides with salt and pepper. Dip each pork chop into egg, then press both sides into Parmesan. Place pork chops into ungreased air fryer basket. Adjust the temperature to 204°C and air fry for 12 minutes, turning chops halfway through cooking. Pork chops will be golden and have an internal temperature of at least 64°C when done. Serve warm.

Chapter 10 Desserts

Cream-Filled Sandwich Cookies

Prep time: 8 minutes | Cook time: 8 minutes | Makes 8 cookies

Coconut, or avocado oil, for spraying	60 ml milk
1 tube croissant dough	8 cream-filled sandwich biscuits
	1 tablespoon icing sugar

Line the air fryer basket with baking paper, and spray lightly with oil. Unroll the dough and cut it into 8 triangles. Lay out the triangles on a work surface. Pour the milk into a shallow bowl. Quickly dip each cookie in the milk, then place in the center of a dough triangle. Wrap the dough around the cookie, cutting off any excess and pinching the edges to seal. You may be able to combine the excess dough to cover additional cookies, if desired. Place the wrapped cookies in the prepared basket, seam-side down, and spray lightly with oil. Bake at 176°C for 4 minutes, flip, spray with oil, and cook for another 3 to 4 minutes, or until puffed and golden brown. Dust with the icing sugar and serve.

Cinnamon Cupcakes with Cream Cheese Frosting

Prep time: 10 minutes | Cook time: 20 to 25 minutes | Serves 6

50 g almond flour, plus 2 tablespoons	½ teaspoon vanilla extract
2 tablespoons low-carb vanilla protein powder	2 tablespoons heavy cream
	Cream Cheese Frosting:
⅛ teaspoon salt	110 g cream cheese, softened
1 teaspoon baking powder	2 tablespoons unsalted butter, softened
¼ teaspoon ground cinnamon	½ teaspoon vanilla extract
55 g unsalted butter	2 tablespoons powdered sweetener
25 g powdered sweetener	
2 eggs	1 to 2 tablespoons heavy cream

Preheat the air fryer to 160°C. Lightly coat 6 silicone muffin cups with oil and set aside. In a medium bowl, combine the almond flour, protein powder, salt, baking powder, and cinnamon; set aside. In a stand mixer fitted with a paddle attachment, beat the butter and sweetener until creamy. Add the eggs, vanilla, and heavy cream, and beat again until thoroughly combined. Add half the flour mixture at a time to the butter mixture, mixing after each addition, until you have a smooth, creamy batter. Divide the batter evenly among the muffin cups, filling each one about three-fourths full. Arrange the muffin cups in the air fryer and air fry for 20 to 25 minutes, or until a toothpick inserted into the center of a cupcake comes out clean. Transfer the cupcakes to a rack and let cool completely. To make the cream cheese frosting: In a stand mixer fitted with a paddle attachment, beat the cream cheese, butter, and vanilla until fluffy. Add the sweetener and mix again until thoroughly combined. With the mixer running, add the heavy cream a tablespoon at a time until the frosting is smooth and creamy. Frost the cupcakes as desired.

Old-Fashioned Fudge Pie

Prep time: 15 minutes | Cook time: 25 to 30 minutes | Serves 8

300 g granulated sugar	12 tablespoons unsalted butter, melted
40 g unsweetened cocoa powder	1½ teaspoons vanilla extract
70 g self-raising flour	1 (9-inch) unbaked piecrust
3 large eggs, unbeaten	30 g icing sugar (optional)

In a medium bowl, stir together the sugar, cocoa powder, and flour. Stir in the eggs and melted butter. Stir in the vanilla. Preheat the air fryer to 176°C. Pour the chocolate filing into the crust. Cook for 25 to 30 minutes, stirring every 10 minutes, until a knife inserted into the middle comes out clean. Let sit for 5 minutes before dusting with icing sugar (if using) to serve.

Vanilla and Cardamon Walnuts Tart

Prep time: 5 minutes | Cook time: 13 minutes | Serves 6

240 ml coconut milk	2 eggs
60 g walnuts, ground	1 teaspoon vanilla essence
60 g powdered sweetener	¼ teaspoon ground cardamom
55 g almond flour	¼ teaspoon ground cloves
55 g butter, at room temperature	Cooking spray

Preheat the air fryer to 184°C. Coat a baking pan with cooking spray. Combine all the ingredients except the oil in a large bowl and stir until well blended. Spoon the batter mixture into the baking pan. Bake in the preheated air fryer for approximately 13 minutes. Check the tart for doneness: If a toothpick inserted into the center of the tart comes out clean, it's done. Remove from the air fryer and place on a wire rack to cool. Serve immediately.

Apple Wedges with Apricots

Prep time: 5 minutes | Cook time: 15 to 18 minutes | Serves 4

4 large apples, peeled and sliced into 8 wedges	1 to 2 tablespoons granulated sugar
2 tablespoons light olive oil	½ teaspoon ground cinnamon
95 g dried apricots, chopped	

Preheat the air fryer to 180ºC. Toss the apple wedges with the olive oil in a mixing bowl until well coated. Place the apple wedges in the air fryer basket and air fry for 12 to 15 minutes. Sprinkle with the dried apricots and air fry for another 3 minutes. Meanwhile, thoroughly combine the sugar and cinnamon in a small bowl. Remove the apple wedges from the basket to a plate. Serve sprinkled with the sugar mixture.

Cinnamon and Pecan Pie

Prep time: 10 minutes | Cook time: 25 minutes | Serves 4

1 pack shortcrust pastry	⅛ teaspoon nutmeg
½ teaspoons cinnamon	3 tablespoons melted butter, divided
¾ teaspoon vanilla extract	
2 eggs	2 tablespoons sugar
175 ml maple syrup	65 g chopped pecans

Preheat the air fryer to 188ºC. In a small bowl, coat the pecans in 1 tablespoon of melted butter. Transfer the pecans to the air fryer and air fry for about 10 minutes. Put the pie dough in a greased pie pan, trim off the excess and add the pecans on top. In a bowl, mix the rest of the ingredients. Pour this over the pecans. Put the pan in the air fryer and bake for 25 minutes. Serve immediately.

Eggless Farina Cake

Prep time: 30 minutes | Cook time: 25 minutes | Serves 6

Vegetable oil	55 g ghee, butter or coconut oil, melted
470 ml hot water	
165 g chopped dried fruit, such as apricots, golden raisins, figs, and/or dates	2 tablespoons plain Greek yogurt, or sour cream
	1 teaspoon ground cardamom
165 g very fine semolina	1 teaspoon baking powder
235 ml milk	½ teaspoon baking soda
200 g granulated sugar	Whipped cream, for serving

Grease a baking pan with vegetable oil. In a small bowl, combine the hot water and dried fruit; set aside for 20 minutes to plump up the fruit. Meanwhile, in a large bowl, whisk together the semolina, milk, sugar, ghee, yogurt and cardamom. Let stand for 20 minutes to allow the semolina to soften and absorb some of the liquid. Drain the dried fruit, and gently stir it into the batter. Add the baking powder and baking soda and stir until thoroughly combined. Pour the batter into the prepared pan. Set the pan in the air fryer basket. Set the air fryer to 164ºC, and cook for 25 minutes, or until a toothpick inserted into the center of the cake comes out clean. Let the cake cool in the pan on a wire rack for 10 minutes. Remove the cake from the pan and let cool on the rack for 20 minutes before slicing. Slice and serve topped with whipped cream.

Lime Bars

Prep time: 10 minutes | Cook time: 33 minutes | Makes 12 bars

140 g blanched finely ground almond flour, divided	4 tablespoons salted butter, melted
75 g powdered sweetener, divided	120 ml fresh lime juice
	2 large eggs, whisked

In a medium bowl, mix together 110 g flour, 25 g sweetener, and butter. Press mixture into bottom of an ungreased round nonstick cake pan. Place pan into air fryer basket. Adjust the temperature to 148ºC and bake for 13 minutes. Crust will be brown and set in the middle when done. Allow to cool in pan 10 minutes. In a medium bowl, combine remaining flour, remaining sweetener, lime juice, and eggs. Pour mixture over cooled crust and return to air fryer for 20 minutes. Top will be browned and firm when done. Let cool completely in pan, about 30 minutes, then chill covered in the refrigerator 1 hour. Serve chilled.

Hazelnut Butter Cookies

Prep time: 30 minutes | Cook time: 20 minutes | Serves 10

4 tablespoons liquid monk fruit, or agave syrup	190 g almond flour
	110 g coconut flour
65 g hazelnuts, ground	55 g granulated sweetener
110 g unsalted butter, room temperature	2 teaspoons ground cinnamon

Firstly, cream liquid monk fruit with butter until the mixture becomes fluffy. Sift in both types of flour. Now, stir in the hazelnuts. Now, knead the mixture to form a dough; place in the refrigerator for about 35 minutes. To finish, shape the prepared dough into the bite-sized balls; arrange them on a baking dish; flatten the balls using the back of a spoon. Mix granulated sweetener with ground cinnamon. Press your cookies in the cinnamon mixture until they are completely covered. Bake the cookies for 20 minutes at 154ºC. Leave them to cool for about 10 minutes before transferring them to a wire rack. Bon appétit!

Berry Crumble

Prep time: 10 minutes | Cook time: 15 minutes | Serves 4

For the Filling:
300 g mixed berries
2 tablespoons sugar
1 tablespoon cornflour
1 tablespoon fresh lemon juice
For the Topping:
30 g plain flour

20 g rolled oats
1 tablespoon granulated sugar
2 tablespoons cold unsalted butter, cut into small cubes
Whipped cream or ice cream (optional)

Preheat the air fryer to 204°C. For the filling: In a round baking pan, gently mix the berries, sugar, cornflour, and lemon juice until thoroughly combined. For the topping: In a small bowl, combine the flour, oats, and sugar. Stir the butter into the flour mixture until the mixture has the consistency of breadcrumbs. Sprinkle the topping over the berries. Put the pan in the air fryer basket and air fry for 15 minutes. Let cool for 5 minutes on a wire rack. Serve topped with whipped cream or ice cream, if desired.

Coconut Muffins

Prep time: 5 minutes | Cook time: 25 minutes | Serves 5

55 g coconut flour
2 tablespoons cocoa powder
3 tablespoons granulated sweetener

1 teaspoon baking powder
2 tablespoons coconut oil
2 eggs, beaten
50 g desiccated coconut

In the mixing bowl, mix all ingredients. Then pour the mixture into the molds of the muffin and transfer in the air fryer basket. Cook the muffins at 176°C for 25 minutes.

Bourbon Bread Pudding

Prep time: 10 minutes | Cook time: 20 minutes | Serves 4

3 slices whole grain bread, cubed
1 large egg
240 ml whole milk
2 tablespoons bourbon, or peach juice

½ teaspoons vanilla extract
4 tablespoons maple syrup, divided
½ teaspoons ground cinnamon
2 teaspoons sparkling sugar

Preheat the air fryer to 132°C. Spray a baking pan with nonstick cooking spray, then place the bread cubes in the pan. In a medium bowl, whisk together the egg, milk, bourbon, vanilla extract, 3 tablespoons of maple syrup, and cinnamon. Pour the egg mixture over the bread and press down with a spatula to coat all the bread, then sprinkle the sparkling sugar on top and bake for 20 minutes. Remove the pudding from the air fryer and allow to cool in the pan on a wire rack for 10 minutes. Drizzle the remaining 1 tablespoon of maple syrup on top. Slice and serve warm.

Shortcut Spiced Apple Butter

Prep time: 5 minutes | Cook time: 1 hour | Makes 1¼ cups

Cooking spray
500 g store-bought unsweetened applesauce
130 g packed light brown sugar
3 tablespoons fresh lemon juice

½ teaspoon kosher, or coarse sea salt
¼ teaspoon ground cinnamon
⅛ teaspoon ground allspice

Spray a cake pan with cooking spray. Whisk together all the ingredients in a bowl until smooth, then pour into the greased pan. Set the pan in the air fryer and bake at 172°C until the apple mixture is caramelized, reduced to a thick purée, and fragrant, about 1 hour. Remove the pan from the air fryer, stir to combine the caramelized bits at the edge with the rest, then let cool completely to thicken. Scrape the apple butter into a jar and store in the refrigerator for up to 2 weeks.

Kentucky Chocolate Nut Pie

Prep time: 20 minutes | Cook time: 25 minutes | Serves 8

2 large eggs, beaten
75 g unsalted butter, melted
200 g granulated sugar
60 g plain flour
190 g coarsely chopped pecans

170 g milk chocolate chips
2 tablespoons bourbon, or peach juice
1 (9-inch) unbaked piecrust

In a large bowl, stir together the eggs and melted butter. Add the sugar and flour and stir until combined. Stir in the pecans, chocolate chips, and bourbon until well mixed. Using a fork, prick holes in the bottom and sides of the pie crust. Pour the pie filling into the crust. Preheat the air fryer to 176°C. Cook for 25 minutes, or until a knife inserted into the middle of the pie comes out clean. Let set for 5 minutes before serving.

S'mores

Prep time: 5 minutes | Cook time: 30 seconds | Makes 8 s'mores

Coconut, or avocado oil, for spraying
8 digestive biscuits

2 (45 g) chocolate bars
4 large marshmallows

Line the air fryer basket with baking paper and spray lightly with oil. Place 4 biscuits into the prepared basket. Break the chocolate bars in half, and place 1/2 on top of each biscuit. Top with 1 marshmallow. Air fry at 188°C for 30 seconds, or until the marshmallows are puffed, golden brown and slightly melted. Top with the remaining biscuits and serve.

Pretzels

Prep time: 10 minutes | Cook time: 10 minutes | Serves 6

335 g shredded Mozzarella cheese

110 g blanched finely ground almond flour

2 tablespoons salted butter,

melted, divided

50 g granular sweetener, divided

1 teaspoon ground cinnamon

Place Mozzarella, flour, 1 tablespoon butter, and 2 tablespoons sweetener in a large microwave-safe bowl. Microwave on high 45 seconds, then stir with a fork until a smooth dough ball forms. Separate dough into six equal sections. Gently roll each section into a 12-inch rope, then fold into a pretzel shape. Place pretzels into ungreased air fryer basket. Adjust the temperature to 188°C and set the timer for 8 minutes, turning pretzels halfway through cooking. In a small bowl, combine remaining butter, remaining sweetener, and cinnamon. Brush ½ mixture on both sides of pretzels. Place pretzels back into air fryer and cook an additional 2 minutes. Transfer pretzels to a large plate. Brush on both sides with remaining butter mixture, then let cool 5 minutes before serving.

Chocolate Chip Pecan Biscotti

Prep time: 15 minutes | Cook time: 20 to 22 minutes | Serves 10

135 g finely ground blanched almond flour

¾ teaspoon baking powder

½ teaspoon xanthan gum

¼ teaspoon sea salt

3 tablespoons unsalted butter, at room temperature

35 g powdered sweetener

1 large egg, beaten

1 teaspoon pure vanilla extract

50 g chopped pecans

40 g organic chocolate chips,

Melted organic chocolate chips and chopped pecans, for topping (optional)

In a large bowl, combine the almond flour, baking powder, xanthan gum, and salt. Line a cake pan that fits inside your air fryer with baking paper. In the bowl of a stand mixer, beat together the butter and powdered sweetener. Add the beaten egg and vanilla and beat for about 3 minutes. Add the almond flour mixture to the butter and egg mixture; beat until just combined. Stir in the pecans and chocolate chips. Transfer the dough to the prepared pan and press it into the bottom. Set the air fryer to 164°C and bake for 12 minutes. Remove from the air fryer and let cool for 15 minutes. Using a sharp knife, cut the cookie into thin strips, then return the strips to the cake pan with the bottom sides facing up. Set the air fryer to 148°C. Bake for 8 to 10 minutes. Remove from the air fryer and let cool completely on a wire rack. If desired, dip one side of each biscotti piece into melted chocolate chips, and top with chopped pecans.

Breaded Bananas with Chocolate Topping

Prep time: 10 minutes | Cook time: 10 minutes | Serves 6

40 g cornflour

25 g plain breadcrumbs

1 large egg, beaten

3 bananas, halved crosswise

Cooking spray

Chocolate sauce, for serving

Preheat the air fryer to 176°C. Place the cornflour, breadcrumbs, and egg in three separate bowls. Roll the bananas in the cornstarch, then in the beaten egg, and finally in the breadcrumbs to coat well. Spritz the air fryer basket with the cooking spray. Arrange the banana halves in the basket and mist them with the cooking spray. Air fry for 5 minutes. Flip the bananas and continue to air fry for another 2 minutes. Remove the bananas from the basket to a serving plate. Serve with the chocolate sauce drizzled over the top.

Molten Chocolate Almond Cakes

Prep time: 5 minutes | Cook time: 13 minutes | Serves 3

Butter and flour for the ramekins

110 g bittersweet chocolate, chopped

110 gunsalted butter

2 eggs

2 egg yolks

50 g granulated sugar

½ teaspoon pure vanilla extract,

or almond extract

1 tablespoon plain flour

3 tablespoons ground almonds

8 to 12 semisweet chocolate discs (or 4 chunks of chocolate)

Cocoa powder or icing sugar, for dusting

Toasted almonds, coarsely chopped

Butter and flour three (170 g) ramekins. (Butter the ramekins and then coat the butter with flour by shaking it around in the ramekin and dumping out any excess.) Melt the chocolate and butter together, either in the microwave or in a double boiler. In a separate bowl, beat the eggs, egg yolks and sugar together until light and smooth. Add the vanilla extract. Whisk the chocolate mixture into the egg mixture. Stir in the flour and ground almonds. Preheat the air fryer to 164°C. Transfer the batter carefully to the buttered ramekins, filling halfway. Place two or three chocolate discs in the center of the batter and then fill the ramekins to ½-inch below the top with the remaining batter. Place the ramekins into the air fryer basket and air fry for 13 minutes. The sides of the cake should be set, but the centers should be slightly soft. Remove the ramekins from the air fryer and let the cakes sit for 5 minutes. (If you'd like the cake a little less molten, air fry for 14 minutes and let the cakes sit for 4 minutes.) Run a butter knife around the edge of the ramekins and invert the cakes onto a plate. Lift the ramekin off the plate slowly and carefully so that the cake doesn't break. Dust with cocoa powder or icing sugar and serve with a scoop of ice cream and some coarsely chopped toasted almonds.

Almond Butter Cookie Balls

Prep time: 5 minutes | Cook time: 10 minutes |
Makes 10 balls

70 g almond butter
1 large egg
1 teaspoon vanilla extract
30 g low-carb protein powder
30 g powdered sweetener

25 g desiccated unsweetened coconut
40 g low-carb, sugar-free chocolate chips
½ teaspoon ground cinnamon

In a large bowl, mix almond butter and egg. Add in vanilla, protein powder, and sweetener. Fold in coconut, chocolate chips, and cinnamon. Roll into 1-inch balls. Place balls into a round baking pan and put into the air fryer basket. Adjust the temperature to 160ºC and bake for 10 minutes. Allow to cool completely. Store in an airtight container in the refrigerator up to 4 days.

Almond-Roasted Pears

Prep time: 10 minutes | Cook time: 15 to 20 minutes
| Serves 4

Yogurt Topping:
140-170 g pot vanilla Greek yogurt
¼ teaspoon almond flavoring

2 whole pears
4 crushed Biscoff biscuits
1 tablespoon flaked almonds
1 tablespoon unsalted butter

Stir the almond flavoring into yogurt and set aside while preparing pears. Halve each pear and spoon out the core. Place pear halves in air fryer basket, skin side down. Stir together the crushed biscuits and almonds. Place a quarter of this mixture into the hollow of each pear half. Cut butter into 4 pieces and place one piece on top of biscuit mixture in each pear. Roast at 184ºC for 15 to 20 minutes, or until pears have cooked through but are still slightly firm. Serve pears warm with a dollop of yogurt topping.

Fried Oreos

Prep time: 7 minutes | Cook time: 6 minutes per
batch | Makes 12 cookies

Coconut, or avocado oil for misting, or nonstick spray
120 g ready-made pancake mix
1 teaspoon vanilla extract
120 ml water, plus 2

tablespoons
12 Oreos or other chocolate sandwich biscuits
1 tablespoon icing sugar

Spray baking pan with oil or nonstick spray and place in basket. Preheat the air fryer to 200ºC. In a medium bowl, mix together the pancake mix, vanilla, and water. Dip 4 cookies in batter and place in baking pan. Cook for 6 minutes, until browned. Repeat steps 4 and 5 for the remaining cookies. Sift icing sugar over warm cookies.

Crustless Peanut Butter Cheesecake

Prep time: 10 minutes | Cook time: 10 minutes | Serves 2

110 g cream cheese, softened
2 tablespoons powdered sweetener
1 tablespoon all-natural, no-

sugar-added peanut butter
½ teaspoon vanilla extract
1 large egg, whisked

In a medium bowl, mix cream cheese and sweetener until smooth. Add peanut butter and vanilla, mixing until smooth. Add egg and stir just until combined. Spoon mixture into an ungreased springform pan and place into air fryer basket. Adjust the temperature to 148ºC and bake for 10 minutes. Edges will be firm, but center will be mostly set with only a small amount of jiggle when done. Let pan cool at room temperature 30 minutes, cover with plastic wrap, then place into refrigerator at least 2 hours. Serve chilled.

Vanilla Scones

Prep time: 20 minutes | Cook time: 10 minutes | Serves 6

110 g coconut flour
½ teaspoon baking powder
1 teaspoon apple cider vinegar
2 teaspoons mascarpone
60 ml heavy cream

1 teaspoon vanilla extract
1 tablespoon granulated sweetener
Cooking spray

In the mixing bowl, mix coconut flour with baking powder, apple cider vinegar, mascarpone, heavy cream, vanilla extract, and sweetener. Knead the dough and cut into scones. Then put them in the air fryer basket and sprinkle with cooking spray. Cook the vanilla scones at 185ºC for 10 minutes.

Coconut-Custard Pie

Prep time: 10 minutes | Cook time: 20 to 23 minutes
| Serves 4

240 ml milk
50 g granulated sugar, plus 2 tablespoons
30 g scone mix
1 teaspoon vanilla extract

2 eggs
2 tablespoons melted butter
Cooking spray
50 g desiccated, sweetened coconut

Place all ingredients except coconut in a medium bowl. Using a hand mixer, beat on high speed for 3 minutes. Let sit for 5 minutes. Preheat the air fryer to 164ºC. Spray a baking pan with cooking spray and place pan in air fryer basket. Pour filling into pan and sprinkle coconut over top. Cook pie for 20 to 23 minutes or until center sets.

Pears with Honey-Lemon Ricotta

Prep time: 10 minutes | Cook time: 8 minutes | Serves 4

2 large Bartlett pears

3 tablespoons butter, melted

3 tablespoons brown sugar

½ teaspoon ground ginger

¼ teaspoon ground cardamom

125 g full-fat ricotta cheese

1 tablespoon honey, plus additional for drizzling

1 teaspoon pure almond extract

1 teaspoon pure lemon extract

Peel each pear and cut in half, lengthwise. Use a melon baller to scoop out the core. Place the pear halves in a medium bowl, add the melted butter, and toss. Add the brown sugar, ginger, and cardamom; toss to coat. Place the pear halves, cut side down, in the air fryer basket. Set the air fryer to 192°C cooking for 8 to 10 minutes, or until the pears are lightly browned and tender, but not mushy. Meanwhile, in a medium bowl, combine the ricotta, honey, and almond and lemon extracts. Beat with an electric mixer on medium speed until the mixture is light and fluffy, about 1 minute. To serve, divide the ricotta mixture among four small shallow bowls. Place a pear half, cut side up, on top of the cheese. Drizzle with additional honey and serve.

Lemon Raspberry Muffins

Prep time: 5 minutes | Cook time: 15 minutes | Serves 6

220 g almond flour

75 g powdered sweetener

1¼ teaspoons baking powder

⅓ teaspoon ground allspice

⅓ teaspoon ground star anise

½ teaspoon grated lemon zest

¼ teaspoon salt

2 eggs

240 ml sour cream

120 ml coconut oil

60 g raspberries

Preheat the air fryer to 176°C. Line a muffin pan with 6 paper cases. In a mixing bowl, mix the almond flour, sweetener, baking powder, allspice, star anise, lemon zest, and salt. In another mixing bowl, beat the eggs, sour cream, and coconut oil until well mixed. Add the egg mixture to the flour mixture and stir to combine. Mix in the raspberries. Scrape the batter into the prepared muffin cups, filling each about three-quarters full. Bake for 15 minutes, or until the tops are golden and a toothpick inserted in the middle comes out clean. Allow the muffins to cool for 10 minutes in the muffin pan before removing and serving.

Printed in Great Britain
by Amazon